A Complete Session of Meditation

The Theory and Practice of Kagyu-nyingma Meditation from Shamatha to Dzogchen

By Tony Duff
Padma Karpo Translation Committee

Copyright © 2014 Tony Duff. All rights reserved. No portion of this book may be reproduced in any form or by any means, electronic or mechanical, including photography, recording, or by any information storage or retrieval system or technologies now known or later developed, without permission in writing from the publisher.

First edition, June, 2007
Second edition February, 2014
ISBN paper book: 978-9937-572-71-2
ISBN e-book: 978-9937-572-72-9

Janson typeface with diacritical marks and
Tibetan Classic Chogyal typeface
designed and created by Tony Duff,

Produced, Printed, and Published by
Padma Karpo Translation Committee
P.O. Box 4957
Kathmandu
NEPAL

Committee members for this book: translation and composition, Tony Duff; editorial, Hayley Curry, Tom Anderson, Jason Watkin; cover design, George Romvari.

Web-site and e-mail contact through:
http://www.pktc.org/pktc
or search Padma Karpo Translation Committee on the web.

Contents

Introduction v

I. Possibilities
Your Enlightened Core 3
Great Beings Talk About the Enlightened Core 9

II. Overview
Overview of the Path of Meditation 25

III. A Complete Session of Meditation
Preparations:
> Taking Refuge and Arousing Enlightenment Mind 35

Main Practices:
> Development of Insight into Reality Through the Practices of Shamatha and Vipashyana 59
> The Key Points of the Body: Posture 65
> The Key Points of Mind: Shamatha 67

The Key Points of Mind: Vipashyana: The Two
    Truths and Emptiness 85
The Key Points of Mind: Vipashyana: Emptiness
    Progressively Understood Through the Four
    Schools of Buddhist Philosophy 107
The Key Points of Mind: Vipashyana: Emptiness
    Known Through Examination of Time 121
The Key Points of Mind: Vajra Vehicle
    Meditations on Reality 123

Conclusion:

Dedication, The Seal 139

GLOSSARY 143

ABOUT THE AUTHOR, PADMA KARPO
TRANSLATION COMMITTEE, AND THEIR
SUPPORTS FOR STUDY 167

INDEX 173

Introduction

One simple truth pervades this book—you possess a mind that is rotten on the surface but fine at its core. Meditation is the way to get back to that core. This book presents the sequence of meditations used in the Tibetan Buddhist system to return to your mind's healthy core.

The Buddha's basic message is that each person is inherently sane and can return to that sanity through straightforward meditation practices. Unfortunately, the simple message of sanity is sometimes obscured by the approach of some of the Tibetan Buddhist traditions who emphasize a scholarly type of meditation. These traditions are perfectly correct in their presentation of Buddhist practice and their way can be effective because of the modern population's highly developed intellect. Equally though, their style of intellectual investigation can sometimes become poison rather than medicine for modern minds which are already deeply enmeshed in concept. Their style can unintentionally cause a meditator to become more habituated to the problem mind instead of sending them beyond to the good core of mind.

The Kagyus and Nyingmas, which are two of the four main schools of Tibetan Buddhism, are famous for meditation practice done to cut through the problem mind and penetrate directly to the sane mind which is at the core of every being. I learned this style of practice from Chogyam Trungpa Rinpoche during my twelve years with him and his community in the late twentieth century. Since then, I have spent my life translating for many other teachers of the Kagyu and Nyingma lineages and teaching this type of meditation directly to non-Tibetans.

Mingyur Rinpoche is one of the Kagyu-Nyingma teachers for whom I have translated in recent years and who upholds this direct approach to the mind. He is a popular, upcoming teacher of the Tibetan tradition who has become known for using the vernacular of modern, Western science to teach Buddhism. Early in our work together, I told him that I would make books of his teachings, which he was pleased about. With his encouragement, I combined some of his teachings with many of my own writings and translated materials to produce this book.

In general, there are many levels of meditation practice in Tibetan Buddhism, from the most basic practices that Buddha taught all the way up to the highest practices that were once practised only by a worthy few in secret. The highest practices, known as Mahāmudrā and Great Completion, have become public in recent times. Many on the spiritual path have now heard of them and desire them above all else. Nonetheless, most people need to start with a more conventional level of spiritual practice. If and when they prove themselves worthy, they can then start these higher level practices.

There are many ways to train yourself so that you are ready for the high practices. Some ways focus on making yourself into a good person, spiritually speaking, so that you can proceed further. Other ways actually involve the special techniques of the higher practices. One very skilful approach teaches a practice that fits with the higher practices but avoids revealing the inner secrets of those practices. This universally applicable practice of meditation not only works in its own right but also opens the possibility of proceeding to the higher practices. It is the style of meditation shown in this book, and it is called shamatha-vipashyana. This book teaches a complete approach to meditation at the shamatha-vipashyana level and includes a chapter that describes the style of the higher practices. It is presented according to the Kagyu and Nyingma traditions of Tibet.

About Mingyur Rinpoche and His Teaching Style

Mingyur Rinpoche is the eighth incarnation of an individual named Yonggay Mingyur Dorje who was born in 1628 A.D. He was a Kagyu practitioner who revealed a major set of treasures originally concealed by Padmasambhava called the "Heaven Treasures". As a result, he is also known as Terton—meaning Treasure Revealer—Mingyur Dorje. Traditionally, nearly all treasure revealers belong to and stay in the Nyingma lineage. Mingyur Rinpoche, however, belonged to the Kagyu lineage. His various incarnations since then have been Kagyu practitioners with a strong affinity for the Nyingma teachings. All of the incarnations have been renowned for their high degree of realization.

Mingyur Rinpoche is the younger brother of Tsoknyi Rinpoche. As Tsoknyi Rinpoche's personal translator, I was asked to translate for Mingyur Rinpoche when he first started teaching and accompanied him on his first tour of the United States in the late 1990's. Mingyur Rinpoche and I spent many hours discussing the intricacies of modern physics and biology. I had sufficient mastery of the Tibetan language and Buddhist thought to translate the ideas of Western science, which I had mastered during extensive scientific training, into a language that he could truly understand. Our discussions of various theories and principles became part of his teaching style; he knew that teaching through science was the way to reach Westerners. Soon, I found myself translating the subtleties of Heisenberg's uncertainty principle and other complex theories I had taught him from Tibetan back into English for dharma audiences! I could only marvel at the humor in that. We had an excellent collaboration that seemed to be of great benefit to the audience.

Since then, the scientific approach is still quite evident when he explains reality. I have my reservations about this approach for the reasons mentioned below. Ultimately, as a translator, I have seen that there is not much value in spouting scientific theory to those interested in practising Buddhism. It only serves to reinforce a belief system to which the Western world already clings. It also fails miserably to reach the fundamental point of commonality between the two systems—the development of the mind as a tool for investigating and reaching reality, the great value of Buddhist teaching.

Later, Rinpoche asked me if I would accompany him for a period of years in the West. He had been offered a place at a college and wanted me to go with him as his tutor. By that time, though, I was not convinced that the pure science he was learning was of benefit to the average person in the audience.

I suggested that a more psychological approach, like that of Chogyam Trungpa Rinpoche, would likely be of farther-reaching effect. With that, I made the difficult choice to not go with him.

I believe that a focus on the development of the tools of mind and their uses, expressed in a way that makes sense to a Westerner's rational mind, but without all of the extra scientific theory is of most value when teaching Buddhism. That approach is precisely what this book is about. It shows Buddhism in a way that someone who favours a scientific approach will appreciate but without straying into scientific specifics that detract from understanding.

The Meeting Point of Science and Buddhist Meditation

In my early twenties, I left academia, where I had studied for a Ph.D. and published research papers in molecular biology, to take ordination as a Buddhist monk. As a monk, I received extensive teachings on Buddhist philosophy and practice. I remember how excited I became when those teachings seemed to be connected with Western science. I also remember trying to catch the ear of our very well-trained Tibetan teacher in order to discuss the scientific connection. He showed a complete lack of interest in this connection and was emphatic about the need to follow the meditation instructions he was giving. His dismissal was very disappointing at the time. Nevertheless, I did have faith in his training and committed myself to studying and practising as much as possible, just as he recommended. Now, after many years of practice and study, I clearly see the value of his position. Science is an interesting pursuit that certainly satisfies the intellectual mind and fits well with the rational mind that is the hallmark of modern Western civilization but it fails to uncover the reality of mind.

When I compare my formal training in the sciences with my experiences during formal training in the Buddhist system, I see that scientific discussions of how the brain works and of space and time are not very helpful. They are exciting avenues for discussion and understanding but they often only serve to strengthen beliefs in an external reality, not loosen them. This truth is precisely what my old Tibetan teacher understood. It is popular amongst Buddhists today to point to the findings of physics that show the world to be less than solid. After all, that lack of solidity is what Buddhism is about, isn't it? No, not really. Science has discovered a lack of solidity of the external world that is understood within the framework of dualistic mind. Buddhism, alternatively, reaches the fundamental lack of solidity pervading everything, external and internal, by relying on a non-dualistic way of knowing.

What is important, according to Buddhism, is to develop insight into reality given that reality is connected with mind. In Buddhism, the insight can be developed in a conventional way by developing the critical faculty of rational mind, as is done in Western scientific training. It can also be developed in an unconventional way by achieving direct, non-rational insight into reality, a technique not known in Western science.

In the Buddhist system, the teachings on the conventional way to develop insight are contained in the exoteric teachings of the Buddha, the sutras, and the teachings on the unconventional way are contained in the esoteric teachings, the tantras. Of all these teachings, the very highest ones bypass intellect completely and do not require the development of the critical faculty of rational mind in order to develop insight into reality. For the majority of people, however, the development of insight into reality will require the development of this critical faculty of rational mind.

Modern Buddhists often think that the beauty of an education in Western science is that you can try to understand Buddhist theories of perception or fundamental reality in relationship to scientific knowledge, like how the brain works and how space and time work. Based on my own experience of both worlds, however, I believe that is a major mistake. The value of a scientific education is that it teaches you to think correctly, that it trains and develops your critical faculty of mind. It gives you a tool to carry out an investigation. In Western science, you use that tool to develop insight into the external reality of the material world, but you could also use that exact same tool to investigate reality in the way that Buddhism teaches. Thus, the meeting point of Western science and Buddhism does not lie in examination of fancy theories of perception, space and time, etcetera. It lies exactly in the development of the mental tools needed for gaining insights.

A Western scientific education tries to develop the critical quality of mind in the student by focussing on the development of the ability to reason correctly. A Buddhist education also tries to develop that reason in the student and has more extensive and precise explanations of how to do so. If your critical faculty is to function well, the mind also needs to be calm and one-pointed. Western science has no techniques for the development of that quality other than the general knowledge contained within Western culture of how to relax. The Buddhist system, on the other hand, has extensive and precise techniques for developing that quality of mind. In Buddhism, the one-pointed quality of mind is called "shamatha," literally meaning the ability to abide calmly. The insightful quality of mind is called "prajna" or "vipashyana"—prajna meaning the critical faculty of mind all together and vipashyana meaning the moment to moment insight that leads to obtaining the critical faculty as a whole. This book is about the development of these qualities of mind and their application because, ultimately, it is those qualities of mind that do bring insight into reality and the concomitant development of spiritual qualities.

It is possible to apply these fundamental qualities of mind—one-pointedness and insight—to anything at all. You can even apply them to choosing which toothpaste to purchase when confronted with the vast array of different toothpastes available at your local, Western shop. You could also apply them to space and time, theories of perception, and so on. However, none of those applications of your critical faculty is going to get you out of the particular problems that you face in your life or coming lives.

That very fact is where Western science and Buddhism differ. They are the same in acknowledging that developing the tools that make mind workable and useful is necessary, but the investigations of Western science do not get past the belief that the reality known through the senses is real. Because of this belief, science does not become a liberating study. Buddhism, alternatively, does go all the way through to the most fundamental level of reality, a reality found in connection with mind, and in doing so allows for the possibility of real emancipation from the various problems that come from holding onto some kind of reality.

Some Western Buddhists have become very excited about the scientific discoveries that atoms are nebulous—that they are, at their limit, energy. It has also become popular to set up symposia with the great minds of Tibetan Buddhism to track down this and other items of scientific interest. However, the truth is that the mere mistiness of solidity that Western science has discovered is not at all the reality at which Buddhism is pointing. Buddhism goes much further in its application of the one-pointed and critical faculties of mind. It applies them in a way that leads beyond fixation or any kind of holding to fixed realities at all.

The Style of Teaching Contained Here

Tibetan Buddhism teaches the whole of the Buddha's teaching, which contains both the conventional and unconventional approaches mentioned earlier. Some teachers start with the highest teachings at the unconventional level first, filling in what is needed of the conventional approach as they go. This is called the top-down approach. Others start with the basic teachings and move to the higher ones in a graded way. This is called the bottom-going-up approach.

This book adheres to the bottom-going-up approach. The main section of the book is a complete set of instructions in how to conduct a complete session of the conventional practice of Buddhist meditation. It makes the book an excellent manual for people who want to learn about Tibetan Buddhism and how to meditate.

How this bottom-going-up style of practice fits into the overall system of Tibetan Buddhist practice is important to know. Thus, the instructions on a complete session of practice are prefaced by an overview of the whole path according to the Kagyu tradition and followed by an introduction to the most advanced practices, those of Mahamudra and Great Completion. In this way, the book both puts the instructions into perspective and serves as an overview of the entire system of meditation.

The Possibility

The whole reason for even bothering to meditate or to step onto the Buddhist path is that you do have an enlightened core. Because of it, you can become enlightened. You must understand this at first, so Part One of the book is an explanation of your enlightened core and the possibility for enlightenment that it provides.

Overview of How to Proceed

Once you understand that you do possess such a possibility, it is necessary to follow a spiritual path. Otherwise, the possibility of enlightenment remains only a possibility. Therefore, Part Two follows on from Part One by giving an overview of the whole path to enlightenment as practised by Tibetan traditions of Buddhism in general, but the explanation comes from the Kagyu lineage. All traditions of Tibetan Buddhism are tantric traditions of practice; they follow all three vehicles of the Buddha's teaching but especially the Vajra Vehicle. Thus, the overview of the whole path is given from the perspective that the Vajra Vehicle is, in the end, the main practice.

This overview of the path is joined to a very famous summary of the whole Three Vehicle journey, called the Four Dharmas of Gampopa, a teaching originally given by Lord Gampopa, one of the great forefathers of the Kagyu tradition.

To turn the theory of the path into personal realization, the path must be practised. Practice of the path is centred on meditation, so at the end of the path's overview, Gampopa's instructions on a complete session of meditation are given. These instructions lead on to the rest of the book, which is a presentation of how to conduct a complete session of meditation.

A Complete Session Of Meditation Has Three Parts

Gampopa once instructed Phagmo Drupa, one of his principal disciples, that it was time to go into retreat in the mountains and engage in meditation. At that time, he told Phagmo Drupa to do his sessions with five parts to them. The interchange is recorded in Gampopa's collected works:

> You go to mountainous areas and so on, congenial places where disenchantment can be produced and experience can develop. There you arouse the mind thinking, "For the purposes of sentient beings, I will attain buddhahood". You meditate on your body as the deity. You meditate on the guru over your crown. Then, not letting your mind be spoiled with thoughts, not altering this mind—because it is nothing whatsoever—in any way at all, set yourself in clarity which is pure, vividly present, clean-clear, wide-awake!

Phagmo Drupa attained a very high realization using these instructions so he taught them to all of his disciples. From them, the instructions spread throughout the Kagyu lineages and later became a hallmark of the Kagyu tradition of practice.

The five-part sessions were originally taught as the way to do a complete session of Mahamudra practice, so the system of practice as a whole became known as "Five-Part Mahamudra." The five parts are:

- Arousing bodhicitta (which includes taking refuge)
- Visualization of oneself as a deity
- Supplicating and merging with the guru
- The main practice of Mahamudra
- Dedication

You can read about the entire Five-Part Mahamudra system of practice in *Gampopa's Mahamudra: The Five-Part Mahamudra of the Kagyus*[1].

The advantage of this five-part format for a session of meditation is that every part of the whole Vajra Vehicle journey is included in a session of practice; it makes for a complete session of meditation, which is the theme of this book. A simplified version of this type of complete session of meditation has three parts to it. If the visualization of oneself as a deity and the supplicating and merging with the guru are removed, you have a three-part practice which also makes a complete session. This type of complete session of practice is still a Vajra Vehicle practice because the main practice is Mahamudra.

The main practice of that three-part format can be replaced with a main practice of the Great Vehicle sutra teachings, in which case it becomes a three-part session which is suitable for anyone, including beginners. Atisha and the Kadampa lineage

---

[1] By Tony Duff, Padma Karpo Translation Committee, 2008, ISBN 978-9937-2-0607-5.

that followed him taught just that—a three-part session as the way to do a complete session of meditation in the Great Vehicle sutra tradition. According to the Kadampa teaching, your session must start with the preparations of taking refuge in the Three Jewels and arousing the appropriate motivation. According to the Great Vehicle teachings, this motivation will always be enlightenment for the sake of all sentient beings, known as "bodhicitta." After the preparation, you do the main practice, which will be the Great Vehicle's meditations on emptiness. Following that, a session is sealed with dedication. These Kadampa instructions became part of the Kagyu lineage when Gampopa merged the sutra instructions of the Kadampa and tantra instructions of the Kagyu.

As a result, the main part of this book is a detailed description of how to do a complete session of meditation using the three-part approach according to the sutra level of teachings. It is a level of practice that is suitable for everyone.

The Two-fold Practice of Calming the Mind and Developing Insight Into Reality

A complete session of practice begins with preliminaries, has a main part, and ends with a conclusion. The practice of the main part taught here is the combined meditation of calming the mind and developing insight into fundamental reality. When Buddhism discusses fundamental reality, it states that all things are "empty" and speaks of the "emptiness" of all things. What is this emptiness and why is it so important?

Your surface mind, what most people normally think is their mind, is a mistake. It is a process of knowing that is mistaken because it comes from a fundamental mistake. That fundamental mistake is the invention of a solidified entity for everything that mind knows. The reality of the situation is that these solidified entities do not exist except as an invention of that mistake. The actual situation is devoid of those inventions. As is said in the Buddhist tradition, all things we perceive are empty. They are not there, and that absence itself is called emptiness.

One of the well-known teachings in the Lesser Vehicle points out that any given thing—a dharma or phenomenon—does not have a "self," a fixed entity to it. That is part of the Lesser Vehicle teaching on "non-self." This teaching starts out with rational mind—a name for dualistic mind given because dualistic mind always makes a ratio between this and that; it always sets one thing up against another in order to have its perceptions. The teaching goes on to say that rational mind makes three readily-observable mistakes. First, seeing things as permanent entities when they are really impermanent. Second, seeing things as a singularity when they are a multiplicity. Third, seeing things as independent entities when they are actually interdependent arisings.

The Buddha pointed out that the products of our normal, rational-mind-based perception are always seen in the ways mentioned above. That is how they appear to us immediately, without further thought. If we think about them and use our critical faculty, the prajna mentioned earlier, to later investigate them, we find that they are not the way our immediate perception is telling us they are. Thus, the Buddha used these three mistakes that rational mind makes as a doorway to show how the phenomena of our normal experience are not the way they appear to be. These mistaken phenomena, which are the projections of rational mind, simply do not exist as they appear to us. Their appearance is one that comes from confusion over how things really are.

When you gain insight into the mistaken perceptual process of rational mind, you realize that appearances are not actually existent. Their absence is called their "emptiness." Here, emptiness means that reality is devoid of, empty of, the phenomena that we experience as real. Our perception tells us that things are solidly permanent, that they are a "chunk"—a singularity—sitting there quite independently of anything else. Our rational minds make each phenomenon one hundred percent true and real to us. That is how we understand things to be. In ancient India, this invention of rational mind was called "true existence." True existence is just an invention of rational mind; it is the gadgetry that rational mind uses when it operates the way it does. Phenomena are not truly existent the way that rational mind tells us. This absence of true existence in reality is called just that, "non-true existence" or "lack of true existence" or "absence of true existence." The absence of true existence is the very thing to which "emptiness" points.

When you realize that you are seeing things in the wrong way, your curiosity is invited to investigate how they actually are. For example, when it is pointed out that your mind's idea of things being permanent is a mistake, you start to look into it and find that they are actually impermanent. A similar process takes place with the mistakes of perceiving singularity and independence. If you are fortunate enough to have someone show you how to look even further, it is possible to discover that nothing truly exists. This full discovery has the power to liberate you from the whole mistaken process of mind and the consequent, generally unsatisfactory existence you may lead because of it. Therefore, the teaching on the mis-perceptions of mind becomes nothing less than a doorway to liberation.

Tony Duff,
Padma Karpo Translation Committee,
Swayambunath,
Nepal, February, 2014

Part I

Possibilities

Your Enlightened Core

A person whose mind has not been developed spiritually can be likened to a wild monkey. A monkey can never sit still: the moment it has nothing to occupy itself with, it does something to distract itself. A monkey's mind is so restless that, even when there is no problem, its busy-ness will create a problem. Monkeys are always creating mischief and trouble. If a monkey were put inside a shrine-room, it would drag the cushions around the room, pull the sacred paintings down from the walls, and so on. At some point, it would find a place to rest for a moment but, as it was sitting there, it would feel thirsty so would drink the water from the bowls on the shrine, then it would feel hungry so would get up and eat the shrine offerings. In this way, it would keep itself occupied and satisfied but cause a lot of problems at the same time. Likewise, the ordinary person's mind, which jumps around like a monkey, creates many problems and hardships for the person. The average person does not have a very satisfactory existence because of it.

Is there a real kind of peace for the average person and, if so, where would the peace be found? Peace, real peace, a final kind of ease can be found. The one place that it can be found is in relation to the root of the problems, which is mind.

Everyone does try to find lasting happiness but most people try to find it outside of mind. For example, there are people who are very wealthy and famous. At first sight, it seems as though they have a good situation and are happy because of it. However, when you talk with them, they will tell you about their various problems and some will even say that they have many problems. I have met many people like this—movie stars, and so on.

The root of all happiness and unhappiness is in your own mind. If you can find happiness in connection with your own mind, it will improve your general situation in this life, it will help your later lives as well, and on top of that, it will lead you towards the final state of ease, buddhahood itself. Therefore, you do need to obtain peace based on mind.

This begs the question, "Do I really have peace in mind as part of my nature?" The answer is yes, because your basic nature is what is called "complete purity". This is a purity, a kind of basic goodness. Every sentient being, that is to say, every being with a mind, has, at the core of their being, this purity which is basic goodness. This begs the question, "If I have this kind of very special nature, why is my experience not always satisfactory? Why do I have unsatisfactoriness[2], why do I experience problems? Why am I caught in the vicious cycle of existence?" The answer is that you have not recognised this complete purity, the basic goodness which is your own essence. That is the problem.

You and all other beings do have this good essence and it is the same as the essence of every buddha. It is the potential that can be developed into the peace that belongs to a buddha.

---

[2] Add commentary on unsatifactoriness

However, just having it as a potential is not enough, you have to bring it forth and manifest it fully. To do that, you first have to recognize this essence. Then with that recognition as a basis, you practise meditation. Through that kind of meditation, you can become a buddha, which is the fruition of the path.

The essence of mind is not recognized by ordinary people and they do not advance spiritually because of it. If they did recognize it, they could develop themselves spiritually all the way to enlightenment. These two situations of non-recognition and recognition resulting in spiritual development can be explained using the metaphor of a watch. In this metaphor, you have a very fine watch—one made of diamonds and platinum which keeps the time perfectly—and have it with you twenty-four hours a day. The value of the watch is that you can use it to tell time. However, you do not know that you have such a watch. It is right there for you to look at but, not knowing that you have it, you do not know to look at it. Since you do not know to look at it, it cannot tell you the time and you cannot use it to find out the time. In short, it is of no use to you because you do not recognize the fact that you do have such a watch. Now a good friend of yours, a helpful friend, comes along and says to you, "You do not know the time according to your watch, do you? You have a watch and it is showing the time but it is of no use to you! However, I do know how to look at a watch and tell the time with it and I will show you how to do that". With your friend's help, you first recognize that you do have a watch and after that gradually learn how to look at it. In the end, you are able to use your own watch to know the time as soon as you look at it. At that point, you not only know that you have a watch but you also fully know how to look at it and make use of it.

In the metaphor, the watch is the equivalent of the complete purity which is our essence. In Buddhism, we call this essence the sugatagarbha[3]. Your sugatagarbha is a very precious thing, just like the valuable watch. It is valuable because when it is recognized and brought to full use, you can know everything perfectly, just like a good watch tells the time perfectly. However, at present, just like not recognizing a watch that you are wearing twenty-four hours a day, you do not recognize your own reality, the sugatagarbha, which is with you all of the time. Because you do not recognize it, its value is not available to you. However, you could be introduced to it and be made to recognise it. Just as your helper introduced you to the watch you were wearing in such a way that you recognized the watch, so someone could introduce you to your own sugatagarbha in a way that would allow you to recognize it. The person who can make that kind of introduction is the person who becomes your guru. That person says to you, "Your essence is the complete purity", and introduces you to the reality of your own mind.

Furthermore, when you are first introduced to the idea of having a watch, although you know that you have it, it is not so easy to use it to tell the time. However, if you gradually train in using it, you eventually do understand how to use it and then, in the end, can use it to tell the time immediately and precisely. Likewise, at first, because your guru introduces you to your own reality, you do come to recognize your own reality. However, at that time it is hard to bring it forth into constant manifestation. Nonetheless, if you gradually train in gaining experience of it, it manifests more and more in your being. In the end, when this reality is fully manifest, it is the all-knowing mind of a buddha.

---

[3] See the glossary.

There is another key point here. At some point you have understood that you have a watch and do know how to tell the time with it. However, that did not happen because of a change in the watch; the watch is just the same as it was before. Rather, you have recognized that you do have a watch, and have then learned to use it. The difference in the two situations is that at first you did not recognize that you had a watch and later you did recognize that you had it. Similarly, when you progress along the Buddhist path and finally become a buddha, the essence of mind is not changing, rather the degree to which you recognize it is changing. At first you did not recognize that you had sugatagarbha. Then someone gets you to recognize it momentarily. Then you do the work of following the path: through the practice of meditation, you remove more and more of the obscurity of mind that has been covering it. As you do so, it is revealed more and more and so manifests more and more in your being. When it has been fully revealed, it is fully manifest and that is buddhahood. At that time, all of its qualities—which were initially very hidden—become fully functional, like the watch becomes fully useful after you have trained in learning to use it. At that point, as a buddha, you have all of the qualities of a buddha in a fully functional way.

What is the value of recognizing your own, pure nature and then meditating on that? Because it is your very basis, the very ground of your being, meditation done without an understanding of it cannot be beneficial, ultimately speaking. Meditation done without a proper understanding of it might bring some temporary effects, such as becoming a little more happy or peaceful, etcetera, but cannot bring about ultimate peace, happiness, and the other qualities of enlightenment. Thus, the first step of Buddhist practice altogether is to understand your basis, the ground of your being. The very ground of your being is this pure essence, the sugatagarbha. It might be covered over at present but you can recognize it and then remove its coverings. In doing so, you change from being someone with the potential for ultimate peace to a being that is ultimate peace and moreover, a being who constantly works for the benefit of others in the most effective ways possible.

To summarize, first you recognize your own sugatagarbha then, with that as a basis, you work at gaining experience in it, and eventually you do gain the rank of a buddha. The classical way of saying this in Buddhism is that first you recognize your own ground, then you bring it into manifestation by following the path, and you do that until it has been brought into full manifestation which is the end and fruition of the path and which is none other than buddhahood.

Great Beings Talk About the Enlightened Core

The enlightened core of being discussed in the previous chapter is the very reason for even bothering to do anything spiritually. Therefore, many Buddhist books that deal with meditation start by explaining it. They usually rely on the metaphors and examples given originally by the Buddha himself and his great followers, such as his main disciple Maitreya, who will be the next buddha. For example, the explanation in the last chapter, which was given using the metaphor of a very expensive watch, is actually one of the original metaphors taken and modernized.

What are these metaphors and examples? How exactly did the Buddha and his great disciples such as Maitreya present the enlightened core of being? With exactly the same thought, these questions were taken up and answered by Dolpopa Sherab Gyaltsen in the 14th century C.E. at the start of his famous book *Mountain Dharma: An Ocean of Definitive Meaning*. He started by paraphrasing one of the Buddha's explanations to make the meaning as clear as possible then continued with many quotations from the Buddha and other great beings in the Buddhist tradition. This opening section of his text gives, just as he intended, a very clear view of what the Buddha had to say about the enlightened core of being and how he used metaphor to explain it. Therefore, it is translated here. Dolpopa Sherab Gyaltsen speaks to us ...

Initially then, there is this to understand. In the ground beneath a poor man's house, there is a great treasure of precious things. However, it is obscured by earth and stones seven men deep, so the poor man does not see it nor know of it, and so, not obtaining it, remains in his unsatisfactory state. In just the same way, the great treasure of the qualities of luminosity-dharmakaya is always present in oneself and everyone else but, because it is obscured by adventitious stains, all these beings do not see it, do not know of it, and so, not obtaining it, forever remain in their unsatisfactory state.

They, whoever they are, will, through a holy guru's special oral instructions of special scriptures and perfect reasonings, understand within themselves what is to be attained and what is to be abandoned. This is analogous to beings who possess the divine eye explaining nicely about that treasure due to which they come to know that the great treasure can be obtained, and that the earth and stones covering the treasure must be eliminated. If that knowledge is not clear, they will not obtain the treasure, and, simply by its being clear, they will know to obtain it, which is analogous to the dharma. Having understood the matter like that, they need to get the experience of it, so, in order to dispel adventitious stains in their entirety, they persevere at accumulating completely pure wisdom and what goes with it, which is analogous to the clearing away of the earth and stones seven men deep. What they gain through their experiences is the great treasure which is the final result, the dharmakaya not covered with outflows, and the qualities which are not separate from it, which is analogous to nicely obtaining that treasure of precious things.[4]

At this point you might ask, "From whom do we know about these things?" We know of them from the buddhas and the bodhisatvas who have spoken nicely of them. As was said in the *Tathagatagarbha Sutra*:[5]

> Sons of the family, moreover, it is as follows. To make an example, there is in the ground underneath a poor man's house, under a covering of earth seven men deep, a great treasure of a treasury filled with valuables and gold. That great treasure does not tell the poor man, "Hey! I am here, a great treasure covered with earth!", because the great treasure, being the very essence of mind, is not a being with a mind. The poor man who owns the house thinks like a poor man, and besides, there is no cause for him to think that he is on top of a treasure, so the great treasure in the earth underneath is not heard of, known of, or seen by him.
>
> Sons of the family, likewise there is, underneath the strong clinging within the dualistic mind of every sentient being which is like the house, the

---

[4] The divine eye or god's eye is one of the five eyes, which are five different extraordinary abilities at seeing. The divine eye includes the ability to see under the earth.

[5] ... by the Buddha himself ...

great treasure of the treasury of the tathagatagarbha with the strengths, fearlessnesses, un-mixed qualities, and every other one of the buddha dharmas. However, those sentient beings, due to attachment to visual forms and sounds and smells and tastes and touches, are in an unsatisfactory position and circle around within cyclic existence. Not having heard of that great treasure of dharma, they have not acquired it and are not, in order to totally purify themselves, making an endeavour towards it.

Sons of the family! Then the tathāgatas appear in the world and, amongst the bodhisatvas, fully and authentically teach this kind of great treasure of dharma. They too orient themselves towards then dig for the great treasure of dharma and therefore, in the world, become the ones called "the tathagata, arhat, truly complete buddhas". They, having become likenesses of the great treasure of dharma, have become treasuries of the strengths, fearlessnesses, and the many other dharmas of a buddha and are the sponsors of the treasury of the great treasure who, through their assurance without attachment, become the teachers to sentient beings of the previously unavailable reasonings, examples, reasoning for activities, and activities.

Sons of the family! Moreover, such tathagata, arhat, truly complete buddhas, viewing every one of the sentient beings through the totally purified eye of a tathagata in that way do, in order to thoroughly cleanse their treasuries of a tathagata's wisdom, strengths, fearlessnesses, and un-mixed

buddha dharmas, teach the dharma to the
bodhisatvas.

Also, as was said in the *Highest Continuum Commentary*:[6]

> Within the afflictions, which are like the earth's
>   surface,
> Sits the element of the tathagata like a treasure of
>   precious things,
> Just as in the earth beneath a poor man's house
> There was an inexhaustible treasure.
> The man did not know it nor did the treasure
> Tell him "I am here".
> Like that, the internal essence of the mind is a
>   precious treasure,
> The stainless and not-to-be-clarified dharmata[7],
> Yet, through not realizing it, the unsatisfactoriness
>   of poverty
> Is continuously and always experienced by these
>   nine beings[8].

Just as in a poor man's house there was an internal, precious treasure which the poor man did not know of because it did

---

[6] Now he presents something from the bodhisatvas. *The Highest Continuum* is a text of the master of the tenth bodhisatva level Maitreya's teachings. The teaching was given to the bodhisatva Asaṅga, who wrote a major commentary to it, which is now quoted.

[7] "Not to be clarified" means that the dharmata or reality is pure in itself and needs no cleaning; it only needs to have the adventitious coverings removed.

[8] "Nine beings" is a way of referring to all sentient beings. It means beings in three locations in each of the three realms—desire, form, and formless realms.

not tell him, "I, the precious treasure, am here!", likewise, sentient beings have the dharma treasure in their house of mind and like the poor man do not know of it. However, so that they could obtain it, the rishi[9] took authentic birth in this world.

Moreover, what does the Bhagavat say about this and related matters in *The Mahaparinirvana*? In the version translated by Devachandra it says:[10]

> "Self" means tathagatagarbha. The buddha element does exist in all sentient beings, yet is obscured by the surface appearances of the afflictions. Even as it exists within them, sentient beings are not able to see it. It is like this. To give an example, in a great city, in one poor man's house, there is a treasure of gold which remains unknown. There is a poor woman staying there; she also does not know that there is a treasure beneath the earth of the house. A man who has the method to assist says to the woman, "There is a treasure in your house, but since even you did not know that, how could anyone else know to look for it?" He suggests, "Please seek it yourself", following which she digs inside the house for the treasure and discovers

---

[9] In this case "rishi" means the Buddha.

[10] The *Mahaparinirvana* sutra recounts the situation at the time just before the Buddha's passing, called his parinirvana, and includes his teachings at the time which included teaching on the tathagatagarbha. The Tibetan scriptures contain translations of the sutra made from both the Sanskrit and the Chinese sources, which Dolpopa gives next. He includes the translations from both languages as part of making his point that there is scriptural authority for all of his claims.

it. Having seen it, she is amazed and takes refuge in the person. Likewise, son of the family, the tathagatagarbha is present in all sentient beings, but they are just unable to see it, like the poor woman with the treasure.

> Son of the family, I will now completely teach this point that "Every sentient being has the tathagatagarbha": just as the poor woman did not know it but was taught that she had a great treasure, likewise all sentient beings have tathagatagarbha, but, obscured by the superficies of the afflictions, do not know it, do not see it, so the tathagatas teach that to them and they, happy in mind, take refuge in the tathagatas, and so on.

Similarly, in the *Mahaparinirvana* translated from Chinese, too, there are extremely extensive statements:

> Son of the family, I also say this. Sentient beings having the nature of buddha and the examples of a treasure of precious things in the house of the poor woman, and the vajra jewel which is the forehead jewel of great strength, and the chakravartin king's springs of nectar which are analogies of it ...

and so on. Also in the *Dharani of Entering into No Functioning of Discursive Thought* it says:[11]

---

[11] Skt. Nirvikalpāvatāra Dharaṇi. Tib. rnam par mi rtog pa la 'jug pa'i gzungs. The words "no functioning of discursive thought" are a way of talking about the tathagatagarbha. Discursive thought is the hallmark of the dualistic mind that covers over the tathagatagarbha. The tathagatagarbha itself does not have dualistic mind functioning in it but only as a covering over it. Therefore, in this discourse, the Buddha used the phrase "no function-
(continued...)

Sons of the family, it is like this. For example, under a solid boulder are various, large, precious wish-fulfilling jewels, all luminous; it is a great treasure filled to the brim with precious silver, precious gold, and precious diamonds in separate layers. Then a few people wanting a great treasure arrive and a person who has clairvoyant knowledge of the great treasure says this to them, "Hey you people, under that solid boulder there is a great treasure of precious things completely filled with luminous precious things. There is a treasure of precious, wish-fulfilling jewels under it, nonetheless, what you excavate at first will be only the nature of stone, now dig! When you dig, stone that appears to be silver will appear; you should not take that to be the great treasure, instead just understand it and dig! When you dig, stone that appears to be gold will appear; you should not take that to be the great treasure either, instead again just understand it and dig! When you dig, stone that appears to be various precious things will appear; you should not take that to be the great treasure either, instead again just understand this and dig! Oh people! When you have made an endeavour like that, you will then, without having to put in further effort, see the great treasure of the precious, wish-fulfilling jewels. If you find that great treasure of the precious, wish-fulfilling jewels, you will be wealthy with great riches and have

---

[11](...continued)
ing of discursive thought" as an equivalent to "tathagatagarbha". You will see its use following this.

a high level of things for use because of it; you will have the power to benefit yourself and others.

Sons of the family, in order for you to understand all of the meaning in what I have just said, here is how the example was constructed. The "solid boulder" is a fitting metaphor for the formatives appearing as total affliction[12]. "Underneath, a great treasure of precious wish-fulfilling gems" is a metaphor for the space of no functioning of discursive thought. "People wanting a great treasure of precious wish-fulfilling gems" is a metaphor for bodhisatva mahasatvas[13]. "A person who has clairvoyance of the great treasure" is a metaphor for the tathagata, arhat, truly complete buddha. "The boulder" is a metaphor for concepts that conceive of the nature. "Dig!" is a metaphor saying to practise non-engagement with mentation[14]. "Stone that appears as silver" is a metaphor for the concepts of discursive thought towards the antidote. "Stone that appears as gold" is a metaphor for concepts of discursive thought towards emptiness and so on. "Stone that appears to be various precious things" is a metaphor for concepts of discur-

---

[12] For formatives, see the glossary. "Total affliction" is a name for the state of samsara; it is paired with the term "complete purification" which is the state of nirvana. In other words, the solid boulder is a metaphor for the afflictions which themselves are what cause the ongoing formation of new births in the total affliction of samsaric existence.

[13] "Bodhisatva mahasatva" here means "those great beings, the bodhisatvas" in general.

[14] Mentation is the ordinary, dualistic mind's mentality.

sive thought towards attainment. "Find that great treasure of the precious, wish-fulfilling jewel" is a metaphor for contacting the dhatu[15] of no functioning of discursive thought.

Sons of the family, by that fitting example, one develops an understanding of the entrance into the dhatu of no functioning of discursive thought …

and so on, he speaks of it extensively. These precious extensive texts of the sutra section and the profound commentaries on their intent both must definitely be looked at.

Up to this point, Dolpopa Sherab Gyaltsen has been showing the basic idea that the enlightened core is present in beings. From here he shifts to the next level of presentation which is that the enlightened core has two aspects to it. The first is that beings do have fundamental reality at the core of their being. The fundamental reality is called dharmata, meaning literally the "isness of all things", how all things really are on the inside. The aspect of tathagatagarbha that corresponds to that is called the "natural" type. It is your nature, you do have it. With that as the basis, you can develop spiritual qualities for the benefit of others. Therefore, a second type of tathagatagarbha, called the "developing" type is identified. It refers to the development through practice of the spiritual qualities of a great being. These spiritual qualities are not your nature; you have to do something to develop them. Dolpopa Sherab Gyaltsen continues …

---

[15] "The dhatu" is a name for the tathagatagarbha.

That dharmata of no-functioning-of-discursive-thought and luminosity-dhatu, is the natural lineage[16]. Dependent upon that there is the developing lineage: the seed of emancipation is sown and nurtured and from it special virtue is properly taken up[17]. That produces the form kayas of a tathagata, which is like the production of a resulting, good tree.

Following on from that, the two types of lineage become the basis upon which the wisdom and merit accumulations are practised and by doing so the fruit, the two aspects of dharma-

---

[16] This means that the fundamental reality of your mind is what is left when you do not have discursive thought, with all of the ignorance that causes it, functioning. That fundamental reality is both luminous— meaning not that it is some kind of light but that it knows—and is the dharmadhātu, the zone which is the basis for and within which anything and everything can and does appear.

[17] This means that a person properly takes up the special virtue of the Great Vehicle as opposed to some other form of virtue.

kaya and form kaya are obtained[18]. As was said in the *Great Vehicle Highest Continuum*:

> Like a treasure and resultant tree
> The two lineages are to be known—
> The beginningless nature dwelling and
> The excellence of the authentic takeup.
>
> From these two lineages, the buddha's
> Three kayas are obtained, it is maintained.
> By the first, the first kaya;
> By the second, the later two.

Also, in the *Ornament of the Great Vehicle Sutras*, a text of the Great Vehicle:

> "Natural and developmental and
> Them as support and supported and
> Existing and not existing ..." was said;
> This summarizes each one.

---

[18] Lineage and family are two key terms used when discussing tathagatagarbha. Just as you have a family lineage and because of it have certain, genetically defined possibilities for development, so you have the family and lineage of tathagatagarbha, and have all of the possibilities for development that come with it. In the explanation here, the natural lineage that you have—the fact that you partake of reality—allows you to develop the reality aspect— the dharmakaya—of a buddha and the developing lineage that you have—the fact that you accumulate spiritual goodness based on that nature of reality—allows you to develop the manifest aspects of a buddha that work for sentient beings.

This raises the very important question of whether you have to develop these qualities as a separate task on the spiritual journey or whether it is possible, just by uncovering the reality which is your nature, to obtain all of the spiritual qualities. The message of conventional spirituality is that it is not sufficient just to uncover the reality of your own nature. It says that you have to look into the emptiness which is the hallmark of your own nature on the one hand and that you have to engage in the production of vast amounts of good works on the other. By doing so, you develop the state of complete buddhahood. Unconventional spirituality, the teaching of the tantras, states that there is a more profound possibility, which is that doing the spiritual work of clearing the dirt that covers and obscures the reality nature at the core of being is, in itself, enough.

Dolpopa Sherab Gyaltsen continues on with several quotes to develop this theme then quotes a very popular section of the *Hevajra Tantra* to make the point that, according to unconventional spirituality, the entirety of enlightenment is contained within the mind and nothing more needs to be done than to uncover it:

> ... The worldly realms have the perpetually
> Blissful nature, nowhere else in them
> Is another buddha to be found.
> Mind is the completed buddha itself;
> No other buddha is taught ...

He explains that by saying:

> Through this it is taught that the nature, the luminosity of the mind[19], present in every one of the sentient beings is buddha and is taught that that buddha is obtained just by it freeing from the entirety of adventitious stains.

The four main traditions of Tibetan Buddhism are, in essence, tantric traditions. Therefore, anyone who fully engages in Tibetan Buddhist practice will end up practising the unconventional spirituality of the tantras. There are two ways to do it. One way is to go directly to the practice of the tantras and the other way is to gain a good grounding in the conventional spiritual path in order to be able to enter and practice the unconventional path of the tantras. The next section of the book is an overview of the path of practice for a person whose main practice is the tantras. That is followed by the actual instructions for a complete session of meditation at the conventional level of Buddhist practice. As explained in the introduction, this creates a good foundation for being able to do the unconventional level of practice in which the inner nature of mind is simply uncovered. Because this approach is better for many people, many Tibetan teachers start their students with it before leading them onto the unconventional approach.

---

[19] Again, nature and luminosity are references to the tathagatagarbha which is the enlightened core of what we think of as mind. Our minds are actually bags of complexity built on top of the actual, very simple, nature of mind.

Part 2

An Overview of the Path of Meditation

An Overview of The Path of Meditation

Tibetan Buddhism follows the system of the Vajra Vehicle, that is, it follows the tantric system. According to the Vajra Vehicle, all meditation is contained within two topics, each of which has two sub-topics, making a total of four topics. They are:

1. Preliminaries
    A. The common preliminaries called "The Four Mind Reversers"
    B. The uncommon preliminaries called "The Four Sets of One Hundred Thousand"

2. Main Part
    C. Development Stage
    D. Completion Stage

Their order and the need for each one can be explained using the "Four Dharmas of Gampopa" which are:

May rational mind turn to dharma;
May dharma turn into the path;

May the path's confusion be dispelled;
May confusion dawn as wisdom.

The ordinary person who is not spiritually advanced has a dualistic or rational type of mind which is not capable of embracing dharma because it is not motivated towards dharma. In order for this kind of person to practise dharma, he first has to orient his mind towards dharma, to motivate it so that it wants to embrace dharma. There is a set of four practices that turn the mind away from its ordinary, non-spiritual interests; these practices reverse the direction of mind so that it turns towards and embraces the dharma. Thus, they are called The Four Mind Reversers and are the first topic explained in the whole subject of meditation. They are preliminaries in the overall practice and they are preliminaries which show the way of dharma at the exoteric or common level, so they are called "The Common Preliminaries". This step of the practice is summed up in the first Dharma of Gampopa, "May rational mind turn to dharma".

Once rational mind has been turned around by the four mind reversers so that it does go towards and embrace the dharma, there is still the problem that the dharma which has been embraced is practised but does not always become the path to reality. This is because the practitioner's mindstream is still quite impure and the attempts at practising dharma do not always connect with the actual dharma. There is a set of four practices that purify and prepare the practitioner so that whatever dharma practice is undertaken, it will turn into the authentic path of dharma. These are called the Four Sets of One Hundred Thousand because each of the practices is done one hundred thousand times. They are preliminaries in the overall practice and they are preliminaries which show the way of dharma at the esoteric or un-common or extraordinary level thus they are called "The Uncommon Preliminaries". This step of practice is summed up in the second Dharma of Gampopa, "May dharma turn into the path".

Once the practitioner's being has been prepared like that using the preliminaries, the main practice of meditation has to be done[20].

First mind was changed so that it embraced the dharma, then that dharma was turned into the authentic path, but still there is the problem that although the dharma is an authentic path of dharma, the practitioner is still situated in confusion. The confusion that the practitioner is situated in is called 'the confusion of the path'.

What is the confusion of the path? Because we have become deluded about reality, we have fallen onto the path; the fundamental confusion that we experience due to our delusion is the confusion that we have in being on the path. The confusion that we have in being on the path is the impure appearances of

---

[20] The main practice of meditation in Buddhism in general is the practice of shamatha-vipashyana. It can be done according to the exoteric explanations of the Buddha, which is the way of the sutras, or according to the esoteric explanations of the Buddha, which is the way of the tantras. The Kagyu lineage contains both sets of explanations but is fundamentally a lineage of the esoteric practice of the tantra. The whole practice of tantra is summed up into two stages or phases of practice. The first is called Development Stage and the second is called Completion Stage. Broadly speaking, in the first stage you use your rational mind to create a pure world that is aligned with the wisdom of enlightenment (so it could also be called "Creation Stage".) In the second, you complete that by turning it into the wisdom of enlightenment.

the containers—the external worlds—and the impure appearances of the contents—the body, speech, and mind of the sentient beings in those worlds.

That confusion of the path has to be cleared and, in the Vajra Vehicle, the vehicle that is the practice of the tantras, the method for clearing it is called "Development Stage". Development stage means "to create something". Development Stage clears the confusion of the path by creating a pure vision of your world that is aligned with enlightenment which is put up in place of the impure appearances that you are currently creating with your confusion. The practitioner of Development Stage creates the perception for himself that the container, the outside world, is a pure place—the immeasurable mansion of the deity—and that its contents, the sentient beings, are pure deities within that place. Overall, that creation of pure perception is done in a three-fold way: to purify the confusion of grasping at a body, oneself and all sentient beings are cultivated as deities; to purify the confusion of grasping at speech, all sounds are cultivated as the sounds of the deity; and to purify the confusion of samsaric mind, the activity of mind is cultivated as being inseparable from the enlightened mind of the yidam-deity. This whole step of Development Stage as the clarifier of the path's confusion is summed up in the third Dharma of Gampopa, "May the path's confusion be dispelled"[21].

---

[21] The third Dharma of Gampopa is usually translated into English as "May the path clarify confusion" and this is how Gampopa himself states it in his own words found in his *Collected Works*. However, all of the Kagyu teachers that I have approached or translated for, including Thrangu Rinpoche, Tsoknyi Rinpoche, Adeu Rinpoche, Mingyur Rinpoche, and others say

(continued...)

Development Stage done on the basis of the two preliminaries is capable of overcoming the confusion of impure appearances but is not capable of purifying confusion in its entirety. To purify confusion in its entirety there is still the need for confusion to dawn as wisdom[22]. For confusion to dawn as wisdom, the practice of looking at mind's essence to find emptiness is required. Completion Stage completes the path of practice by doing just that. This whole step of Completion Stage as the step in which everything shines forth as the empty display of wisdom is summed up in the fourth Dharma of Gampopa, "May confusion dawn as wisdom".

Thus, the whole practice of Vajra Vehicle meditation is contained in those four sections and the meaning was summa-

---

[21](...continued)
that it should be "May the path's confusion be clarified". According to them, the term "path", which could have either the commonly understood meaning "the path you follow to return to enlightenment" or "the path of samsara that you fall onto after making the fundamental error of splitting yourself off from reality", has the latter meaning.

How could this major difference of understanding come about? The Tibetan text of the third dharma of Gampopa is condensed and leaves out a key word that would show clearly whether the meaning should be "confusion of the path be dispelled" or "confusion dispelled by the path". In Gampopa's own explanations of it, he makes it clear that it should be understood as "by the path". However, the lineage has instead developed an explanation based on thinking it is "of the path". The lineage explanation is not wrong, though it has become separated from Gampopa's own explanation of it.

[22] Here, "dawn" is a specific, technical term that means "appear in wisdom mind"; it is possibly better translated as "shine forth".

rized by Gampopa in what have become known as the Four Dharmas of Gampopa.

There are a number of ways to do a session of meditation. However, a common way to do it in the Kagyu school is to do each session in five parts. In that case, the entire meaning of the four sections explained above is included in the meditation by structuring the meditation as a five-part session. These five parts are: first, taking refuge and arousing bodhicitta; second, guru-yoga; third, development stage; fourth, the practice of Mahamudra; and finally, dedication and prayers of aspiration. If all five parts are present in a meditation session in succession like that, the session will contain the full meaning of the four topics that contain the whole meaning of meditation and the full meaning of Gampopa's Four Dharmas that sum them up.

Alternatively, the five-part session can be explained as a three-part session without changing the meaning and in that case, a session of meditation practice that contained all three parts would be complete and sufficient. The three parts which make a session of meditation complete are: first to take refuge and arouse bodhicitta; then to do the main practice; and finally to dedicate the merit and make prayers of aspiration. If the main practice is a practice of Mahamudra or Great Completion, then the session will include all of the meaning explained above from a Vajra Vehicle perspective. Alternatively, if the main practice is a practice of shamatha-vipashyana according to the sutra system of the Great Vehicle, then the session will include the entire meaning of practice at that level. Furthermore, whether you are someone who does not want to do elaborate practice, who prefers a condensed or simple style of practice, or whether you are someone who prefers elaborate practice and who has the capability of doing it, as long as your meditation sessions—simple or elaborate—have all three parts, your practice will be complete.

In short, this three-part style of practice can be used at any level of Buddhist practice as a way of making the session a complete session. It is like having a head, heart, and legs: if you do not have all three, you won't be able to arrive at a destination you want to go to; if you have all three, you can go where you want to go. Similarly, in the case of meditation, if you have all three parts together, you will be able to go to complete perfect buddhahood, whether it is through the more common practices of the sutra system or the uncommon practices of the tantric system.

Part 3

A Complete Session of Meditation in Three Parts

The Preparation

Taking Refuge in the Three Jewels and Arousing Enlightenment Mind

Taking Refuge[23]

Essentially speaking, ordinary beings—meaning beings who are not spiritually advanced—are in a bad position. Their lives are unsatisfactory to start with and every experience of unsatisfactoriness usually causes them to react in a way that does not solve the problem permanently but only causes more unsatisfactoriness in the future. Therefore, the Buddha

---

[23] An explanation of taking refuge can be found in many books these days but you might like *Teachings of the Mountain Hermit of Mandong, Taking Refuge and Arousing Bodhicitta Explained According to Atīsha's Lineage* published by Padma Karpo Translations, ISBN 938-9937-9031-8-9. It is a very nice set of teachings from another well-known Kagyu guru of the 1900's. Alternatively, our *Unending Auspiciousness: The Sūtra of the Recollection of the Noble Three Jewels* ISBN 978-9937-8386-1-0 has extensive and practical explanations of taking refuge with sutras from the Buddha and their explanations included.

started his whole teaching by clearly pointing out the situation to ordinary beings and showing them what could be done about it. This initial teaching is called the teaching of the Four Truths of the Noble Ones[24]. In general, anyone who has become a Buddhist is bound by the Buddha's teaching and his whole teaching is exemplified principally by the teaching on the Four Truths. The Four Truths are:

1. The truth of unsatisfactoriness;
2. The truth of source
3. The truth of cessation
4. The truth of path.

Each of them is to be taken as follows:

1. That which is to be understood
2. That which is to be abandoned
3. That which is to be obtained
4. That which is to be relied on

And, to illustrate the four truths, the Buddha used the simile of a body and sickness.

Beings become ignorant of their own, inner nature. When that happens, they develop a complex mind and are known as "sentient beings", beings with a complex, deluded mind. The

---

[24] This is often translated as "Four Noble Truths" but it is well-known from the explanations of the Buddha and from the great Indian pandits in works such as the *Abhidharmakosha* that it means the Four Truths for Noble Beings. It is the Four Truths seen by spiritually advanced beings, the ones who see emptiness directly. Those beings were called "aryas" by the Buddha, meaning "superior" or "noble" in comparison to ordinary beings who have not advanced spiritually to the point where they see emptiness directly.

deluded mind that they have created creates a deluded existence. To them, the existence seems real but it is a fiction. This fictional reality that they have created for themselves is a product of delusion and because of that, it does not work right. They take birth after birth in this deluded state and this whole deluded reality that all of them live in is called samsara or cyclic existence because of it.

Cyclic existence is unsatisfactory by nature. That is how it is. There is nothing about it that is not unsatisfactory. Because all of us have been wandering in this unsatisfactoriness of cyclic existence since time without beginning, the Buddha saw that the truth of unsatisfactoriness would be the easiest of the four truths for us to understand. Hence he taught that truth to begin with. The truth of unsatisfactoriness is something that you have to understand. The example given is that the truth of unsatisfactoriness is like sickness in the body.

When you understand that cyclic existence is unsatisfactory, you naturally inquire as to the cause of that unsatisfactoriness. When you see that it is unsatisfactory by nature you wonder, "What is the cause of this unsatisfactoriness, where does it come from?" It is possible to temporarily alleviate unsatisfactoriness without knowing its source but to really eliminate unsatisfactoriness its cause has to be known fully. A proper understanding of the source is called the truth of source. The truth of source refers to something that has to be abandoned. The truth of the source is like the cause of sickness in the body.

When the source of the unsatisfactoriness is removed, the result is cessation of the unsatisfactoriness. The kind of cessation that comes specifically from removing the source that has been understood in the truth of source is the truth of cessation. There are various kinds of cessation that correspond to levels of spiritual attainment that come through practising the Buddhist path. These cessations have to be obtained. The truth of cessation is like a body which has been freed from its sickness.

Just understanding that cyclic existence is unsatisfactory, that there is a cause of it, and that it can be stopped does not stop it. To actually stop the unsatisfactoriness a method must be applied. The method is called the path, meaning a roadway that leads to a particular place. There are many spiritual practices but not all of them lead to a true cessation. The Buddha explained what practices do have to be followed in order to get to a true cessation and this, as a whole, is called the truth of the path. The truth of the path is something that you have to rely on; you have to apply yourself to it or you will not get anywhere. The truth of the path is like the instructions given to you by a doctor; if you follow them, you will eliminate the sickness from your body and become well.

All in all, if you have a sick body, you will go to a doctor to find the cause and whether or not there is a cure. If there is a cure, you can get better if you follow the methods given to you by the doctor. It is very helpful in the process to have a nurse who has experience with the disease and who can help you on the road to recovery. Similarly, you have the sickness of your deluded existence. The Buddha is like a doctor who explains the illness to you through the teaching of the Four Truths of the Noble Ones and encourages you to follow the path to the end of the sickness. The instructions he gives are called, in ancient Indian tradition, his dharma, his truth, which he gives to you. This dharma of his is the medicine that you have to take to be cured. His followers who have practised the dharma to the point that they have at least escaped from the delusion of cyclic existence can help you on the way because they have experience of the same path. They were called the "sangha" in ancient India meaning "the community". Note that the community in this case does not mean the general community of Buddhist followers but specifically the community of followers who have attained cessation of one sort or another.

They are the ones who can function as a nurse who will help you on the road to recovery.

Every being has problems and every being tries to solve those problems one way or another. Beings always find some other being or some method or something that they take as a shelter that will keep the problems away. Anyone who has decided to follow the Buddhist path makes a commitment to the Buddha, the Dharma, and the Sangha as their shelter from all problems. The Buddha called them the Three Jewels and said they were the place of refuge for all of his followers. Therefore, in the Buddhist tradition, every practice always begins by taking refuge in the Three Jewels. It is usually done by reciting a liturgy such as this, which is common to all Tibetan Buddhist traditions:

> I take refuge in the Buddha, Dharma, and
>   Supreme Assembly
> Until becoming enlightened;
> By the merit from my meditation and recitation
> May I become a buddha for the sake of all
>   migrators.[25]

---

[25] This is a very common liturgy in all Tibetan traditions. It is a (continued...)

Arousing the Enlightenment Mind

Once refuge has been taken, the right approach to the practice has to be aroused in mind. The general approach of a person treading the path to full enlightenment is called "The mind that seeks to benefit others", a name that sums up the mind that has both loving-kindness and compassion for all beings. This approach of seeking to benefit others is part of an even more encompassing attitude which is the very root of the Great Vehicle path to full enlightenment. This attitude is called bodhicitta or "enlightenment mind". The enlightenment mind is the attitude that you are going to attain the enlightenment of a truly complete buddha because you have taken all sentient beings into account and found that doing so is the best way there is to help all sentient beings, including yourself.

The principal cause behind our problems and suffering is the particular type of self-grasping called "self-cherishing". It is the cause of selfishness and many other unpleasant kinds of behaviour. It is a very deep kind of feeling in the mind that wants only what it wants. It wants profit for itself and either actively wants or does not care about loss for others. If you

---

[25](...continued)
Great Vehicle liturgy; the term "supreme assembly" specifically means the sangha of the Great Vehicle. The phrase "meditation and recitation" can be replaced by any of several standard phrases. "Meditation and recitation" is used at the beginning of a session of meditation or deity practice in which mantras will be recited; "generosity and so on" meaning the six paramitas is used in general circumstances; "explaining and listening" is used at the beginning of teaching sessions; and so on.

have that kind of mind, you will never be able to find happiness for yourself, and not only that but others will not be happy because of it, either. It will create troubles for you, your family, your friends, your environment—for everything and everybody. Nothing around it can be at ease. If you have this kind of mind, whoever sees you will not trust you but will tend to see you as a problem and you too will tend to see others as a problem or an enemy, even to the point where you see yourself surrounded by problematic people. In short, it brings many problems. It is like wearing sun-glasses: if you wear blue-coloured glasses, everything appears in a shade of blue.

If you only think about yourself and getting what you want, you will not be able to accomplish your own desires the way you want and in the end will always be at war with yourself. Nothing ever seems to go right to this kind of mind and it is never at peace with itself because of that. It always finds something wrong with what is happening. Say there are two people. One only thinks of himself; he has plenty of anger, pride, and jealousy. The other has loving kindness, compassion, and the mind that seeks to benefit others. If you compare the two, you will say that the one with loving kindness and compassion is altogether a good person. He will always smile at others and they will find him an agreeable kind of person, feeling that he is like a relative. He and whoever he meets will mutually find each other to be pleasant. The other person, the one full of self-cherishing, with lots of anger, and great affliction, will be seen as bad, or at least not good. Everyone will see him that way.

For example, if you only think of yourself and what you want, you might think, "I'll defeat everyone in my way and overpower them, so that they have to do what I say." If you do that, it will not have the intended effect of overcoming your enemies but will only serve to increase their numbers. First you will make one person into an enemy, then another, then another, and so on. At some point, you will fight with them and then they will stay off to one side after that, not liking you. And what will you do to them, if you really decide to harm them? The worst you can do is to kill them; there is nothing more final than that. But there is the problem that, if you kill one person, there will usually be others who come to retaliate, and they will also need to be killed. You could kill them too but then even more will appear in their place. Eventually the whole world becomes an enemy that must be killed. Hitler is the best recent example of this; he started by killing a few people and went on and on till he killed a significant portion of the world's population. He found no peace in this, only anger and other negative states of mind. In the end what did he get? Although he tried to overcome his enemies they actually increased in numbers till nearly the whole world was fighting against him. In the end, he killed himself.

Anger is a problem. The best way to deal with it is not to remove the outer enemy but the inner mind that is creating the enemy. For example, a long time ago there was a cowherd. In those days, cowherds and other very poor people usually did not have shoes. This cowherd wandered around with his cows and, wherever he went, his feet were hurt by the stones on the ground. He thought about it for a bit and decided that, if he were to cover the ground with leather, this would prevent his feet from being hurt so badly. So he spread leather out across the road. Unfortunately, it could only cover a few metres of the road and, when he got to the end of it, his feet were injured all over again. So there is the question: was that the best way to deal with it? Of course, the answer is no. What he should have done was to cover his feet with leather, for instance by wearing shoes. If he did that, then no matter where he went, the leather would always be there protecting his feet. Similarly, if we tame our own minds, that is, the mind that produces our external enemies in the first place, then our external enemies will automatically be pacified.

The thought that we should fight with our enemies to overcome them only intensifies the situation; it is like thinking that we should cover the whole world with leather to protect our feet. No matter how many external enemies you overcome, you are never finished with dealing with them. It is necessary to understand that the real answer to enemies is to deal with the real enemy, which is the self-cherishing mind.

That then raises the question, what is the opposite of self-cherishing? It is loving-kindness and compassion. If you have loving-kindness and compassion, it will help you and it will help others. Moreover, it will enable you to take care of yourself and to take care of others. In short, it helps everyone.

Some people say that a person with loving-kindness and compassion must be a wishy-washy individual, a person with no inner strength who therefore cannot accomplish anything of importance. However, a person who has loving-kindness and compassion is quite the reverse of that. Such a person has a greater level of mental fortitude and determination to help others and, at the same time, this is mixed with a very spacious mind. This kind of person has confidence and the strength of mind to go forward and do what needs to be done for himself and others. It leads to a level of great bravery and fearlessness in terms of working for others. On the other hand, a person with lots of self-cherishing is someone with a very small mind, a mind that is overly sensitive and cannot bear anything that is done for the greater good. Thus, loving-kindness and compassion is something that we should develop.

Three Successive Levels of Development of The Mind that Seeks to Benefit Others Leads to The Mind of Enlightenment

In the Tibetan tradition of Buddhism, there are two main systems for developing bodhicitta. One is called "The Special Instructions on the Seven Causes and Effects" and the other is called "Equalizing and Exchanging Self for Other". In general, both of these teach a successive development of the mind that seeks to benefit others that culminates in the enlightenment mind. They both develop loving-kindness and compassion first and then bodhicitta following that. Here, the development of enlightenment mind is taught as a progressive development, starting with simple loving-kindness and compassion, followed by limitless loving-kindness and compassion, and ending with actual enlightenment mind.

1. Simple Loving Kindness and Compassion

The first step of the training taught in "Equalizing and Exchanging Self for Other" is to undo our usual approach of seeing ourselves as more important than others and to realize that we are equal with others in terms of our basic goals in life.

The classical explanation of how to do this is to look into what it is that you want most. If you ask yourself what it is that you really want, you will find in the end that you want happiness now as well as the means to get it again in the future, and that you want to be rid of problems now as well as whatever it is that would cause future problems. If you look further, you will find that this is true not only for yourself but for every other being in the world. In other words, this is something that every human at least, and probably all animals, too, in this world would agree to. That is what they want at root and they are all the same in wanting that. The Buddha said that, just as much as you do not want misery and do want a happy state, so every other sentient being—not just the ones on this planet—also want an end to misery and want a state of happiness.

A second way to equalize yourself with others concerns itself with the inner reality of sentient beings that was discussed in the previous chapter. All sentient beings have as part of their being the complete purity that allows them to become buddha; all of them have sugatagarbha at the core of their being. For them, the complete purity that is the sugatagarbha is covered over by various kinds of delusion, nonetheless it constantly provides a natural drive away from the deluded state with its attendant lack of happiness and omnipresent unsatisfactoriness and constantly provides a drive towards the state of enlightenment with its perfect ease and absence of unsatisfactoriness. All beings have this drive towards enlightenment, even though most cannot articulate it. So, if you can get a sense of your own drive to enlightenment, then you can, through this reasoning, understand that all other sentient beings have that exact same drive, too.

When you understand that all beings have an essence which is complete purity, then take delight in that and the possibility of returning to it, just that becomes a basis for both loving-kindness and compassion. Why is that? The Buddha himself said that the principal reason we have the thought of wanting happiness and wanting to be free of suffering is the presence of our inner reality which is completely pure of all of the problematic parts of our existence, which in itself is free from suffering, which is a continual flow of great bliss. This inner reality is present now only as a seed of what it could be and that seed is called our sugatagarbha. Even though it is only a seed, we instinctively feel its presence. We feel that it is our home and long to return to it, which is why we have the strong drive to have happiness and be freed from suffering. The drive to return to it is just like a bird who leaves its nest to forage for food. It has gone from the nest but, no matter how far it flies from the nest, it is always thinking, "Where I am now is not my home, I must return to my home!" Whenever it is away from the nest, it has that strong thought to return to the nest precisely because it takes that as its real home, the place where it belongs. You could say that it gets homesick. Likewise for us, there is a strong urge to find our own home and return to it. At root, we really are the complete purity of the sugatagarbha, and we long to return to it with its absence of suffering and hence its self-contained happiness, a happiness which is free from the spoilage of dualistic mistakes. Everyone wants to return to this, and the sign of that is their wanting to have happiness and wanting to be rid of suffering. Everyone makes efforts to get there, too. However, as we know, some people are successful in their quest, some are partially successful, and many make mistakes about the way to get there even to the point of having a very bad journey. Whether it goes well or not, every sentient being is homesick for the complete purity of their own nature.

When you understand either or both of these points, you can then understand that you are no different from any other being. At that point, there is a natural sense of wanting to give them happiness and its causes and wanting to remove their suffering and its causes. The desire to give them happiness and its causes is the mind of loving-kindness and the drive to remove their sufferings and causes of suffering is the mind of compassion. In other words, the thought, "May myself and all others, every sentient being, have happiness", is loving-kindness and the thought, "May myself and all others, every sentient being, be free from suffering", is compassion.

Thus, according to these instructions, the development of simple loving-kindness and compassion starts by thinking about what you want for yourself. The answer that comes is that you do want happiness, you do not want suffering, and you do want to return to your essence. When you have thought about this carefully and understood it well, you will have a strong sense of wanting to have happiness for yourself, wanting to be free of suffering for yourself, and the drive that we all have to return to our own, good essence with its total ease and liberation. With that, you can begin the cultivation of loving-kindness and compassion and, eventually enlightenment mind.

When you first start meditating on the development of simple loving-kindness and compassion, it is usual to start with beings with whom it is easy for you to develop loving-kindness and compassion. For people of older cultures where respect for parents and close relations with the family are important, this will be your mother, father, relatives, spouse, and so on. This is why prayers concerning the development of loving-kindness and compassion are usually done in relation to mothers as in "All mother sentient beings, limitless as space …". However, Western culture does not always see things that way and quite a few Westerners these days will say that they do not love their mother, etcetera, and say that these meditations are not easy for them. Some even think to themselves, "When will my father and mother die? I just can't wait for that day to happen! When they die I will get all of their money", and so on. That sort of person should use whatever works for him.

When you are capable at the meditation with an easy object, you move to an object that is more difficult, and when you are capable with that, finally you move to an object that is difficult, someone who is your enemy. After practising at that, when you can do the practice with an enemy, you have passed the test. At that point you have graduated from the practice of simple loving-kindness and compassion and can move onto the next level.

Let's make the meditation done with a difficult object, an enemy, an example of how to do the meditation. You cultivate the understanding that your enemy also wants happiness and likewise does not want suffering and therefore is no different from, is exactly the same as, you. When that understanding has strength to it, you will be able to exchange yourself for your enemy, which is a good development. So, you should work at being able to exchange yourself for your enemy. Generally speaking, your enemy has fallen under the control of the afflictions in his own mind and because of that is not really in control of himself. Unfortunately, we tend to think because of that, "Oh, he's a bad person. I could just get happiness for myself; I would be quite pleased to see him destroyed or at least out of the way". But the truth is that if you could overcome him somehow, it would not really help you out. In fact, it would sooner or later, just increase your own problems. And, if you could do something like that, his life this time also would be made harder and less happy. And there is the possibility that he might go to one of the bad migrations in the future.

2. Immeasurable Loving Kindness and Compassion

The second level of development of the mind that seeks to benefit others is the cultivation of the Four Immeasurables. The Four Immeasurables are: loving-kindness; compassion; joy; and equanimity. These are the same as in the "Four Stations of Brahma" taught in the Lesser Vehicle. However, the Four Immeasurables is a meditation of the Great Vehicle done with the thought of every single sentient being, none excluded, where the Four Stations of Brahma is a meditation of the Lesser Vehicle done with a general thought for other sentient beings. This is understood through the change of name of the practice: the meaning of 'immeasurable' used in the name of this Great Vehicle practice is 'all sentient beings', who are immeasurable in number.

The practice of the first immeasurable is to develop the thought, "May every one of the immeasurable sentient beings have happiness". When the thought arises, then immeasurable loving-kindness has been developed. The practice of the second immeasurable is to develop the thought, "May every one of the immeasurable sentient beings be free from suffering". When the thought arises, then immeasurable compassion has been developed.

The meditation on loving-kindness and compassion in this case is the same as for simple loving-kindness and compassion. And the development of the practice is similar: you start with an easy object of the meditation—someone who is close to you—then move onto a middling one, then move to one that is difficult, like an enemy. However, once you have developed yourself in that way, you shift the scope of the meditation and do it for all sentient beings.

"All sentient beings" means all beings who have a dualistic mind and are wandering in cyclic existence because of it. Every one of those other sentient beings is the same as you in wanting happiness and not wanting suffering. Every one of them wants the same thing and wants it just as much as you do. So you develop loving-kindness and compassion for all of them and then join that to the two thoughts given at the beginning of the paragraph.

The third immeasurable is "immeasurable joy". What is that? It is the development of the specific thought, "May all those sentient beings not only have happiness and be freed of suffering but may every one of them abide in the great bliss of the ultimate state which is totally devoid of suffering". You raise this thought and cultivate joy at the idea of every sentient being abiding in that state of ultimate joy—enlightenment—with its absence of suffering. This is opposite to the jealousy which we sometimes have towards others gaining increasing levels of ease.

The fourth immeasurable is "immeasurable equanimity". What is that? It is the development of the specific thought of even-ness towards all sentient beings. Because of developing an even-handed approach to all of them, you wish that all of them equally have the happiness and freedom from suffering that you have meditated on in the first two immeasurables. If you think to yourself, "May these good things come to me and may I not have things that I do not want", or you think, "May it happen a bit better for me than others", then that becomes an obstacle to the development of the first two thoughts. If an even-ness towards all arises without any sense of one being closer and one being further away because of attachment and aversion respectively, then that is called "immeasurable equanimity" and it is the basis for the full development of the other three thoughts.

It is hard at first to give rise to very vast thoughts of the four immeasurables. However, they do come along gradually. If you keep the mind, "It would be good if the four immeasurables developed in me", then they will gradually develop. Sometimes their opposites—anger, jealousy, and so on—will arise and sometimes you might even lose faith in them. That is all right. Just keep the thought that it will be good to develop them and then slowly they will develop.

If you practise with the thought, "I must have perfect four immeasurable thoughts towards all, with no anger whatsoever, no jealousy whatsoever, and so on, and if that doesn't happen, it is not all right", then you will be setting a standard that is too high and the practice will be very difficult to do. There is a story about this. In India, there was a man whose neighbour had a very bad-tempered dog. Whenever the man came and went from his house, the dog growled menacingly and tried to bite him. The dog always acting viciously towards the man, prowling around the man's house and even trying to get inside to bite him. The man threw stones at the dog and beat him with a stick but the situation got worse and worse. Finally, the man could not take it any more and decided to do something about it. He opened his front door a little, to get the dog to come inside. Then he put some very heavy things above the door so that they would fall on the dog when he came in. Having done that, he sat and waited for the dog. After a while, he decided to use his time usefully, so he went to recite some prayers. As he recited them, he got to the four immeasurables, "May all motherly sentient beings, limitless as space ...". He stopped and thought, "Wait, the dog is a sentient being! This won't do!" He thought, "Perhaps I should let go of my anger and meditate on loving-kindness and compassion". But he couldn't do it. He lost his good thought and got angry again. He continued on with his recitations and got to "... have happiness and its cause and be parted from suffering and its cause". At that point, he felt uncomfortable. The dog was a sentient being, after all. So he thought about a solution to the problem. He first thought that perhaps he should give up on the recitations but he thought better of that. He thought and thought, then he got the answer; he changed the verses of the recitation and continued, "May some sentient beings have happiness ...". He spent three hours doing his recitations but the dog didn't come and he forgot about it. When he was done, he thought that it would be a good idea to go for a walk, so he headed out the door. The heavy things over the door fell on his head and stunned him; "What??!", he thought. Then he realized what had happened. He understood that when you make bad thoughts and deeds, they bring bad consequences in return. A strong feeling overcame him and he changed his attitude to the dog. "I really must think of, then cultivate, loving-kindness and compassion towards the dog. If you say, "May all sentient beings have happiness and its cause", then it is not enough only to think that for some of them", he thought. With that in mind, he went and made some really good food for the dog and took it to him. At first the dog was vicious like before but, as the man kept on offering food and talking nicely to it, the dog slowly became more friendly towards him. The dog stopped barking and biting, and, in the end, the two of them became friends and all of the man's earlier problems with the dog disappeared.

That story is a good illustration of how it is. I am sure that, if you try this sort of thing in your own life, you will face many difficulties. However, if you train like that, it will turn out well in the end. There is a quotation from the text *Entering the Bodhisatva's Conduct* that goes with this:

> If you work at acquainting yourself at something,
>   there is nothing
> That does not change to being easy;
> Make efforts to acquaint yourself with this![26]

If you do that, then just as it says, anything will become easy. And if that happens, then there is nothing that will not be easy.

3. Bodhicitta, the Enlightenment mind

The original name for the enlightenment mind is the Sanskrit word "bodhicitta". In it, "bodhi" means the enlightenment which is the attainment of a truly complete buddha and "citta" means mind. The whole means "enlightenment mind".[27]

There are several ways of categorizing the enlightenment mind in order to understand it better. One way is to divide it into two types called, "fictional enlightenment mind" and "superfactual enlightenment mind". The fictional one is a rational mind that thinks, "I want to set every sentient being at the level of a buddha". It functions within and deals with the fictional level of reality. The superfactual one is beyond rational mind; it functions within and relates to factual reality which is superior to fictional reality and is connected with the

---

[26] ... the bodhicitta that puts others above oneself.

[27] See "enlightenment mind" in the glossary for important notes on the meaning.

the inner core of mind that is the nature of enlightenment, also called sugatagarbha.

In the system of instructions called "Equalizing and Exchanging Self for Other", you first equalize yourself with all other sentient beings then exchange yourself for them as described above. However, the natural loving kindness and compassion for sentient beings that arises when you understand that all sentient beings are equal with you is usually not very strong. Therefore, to develop it further, there is a practice called "Sending-Taking"[28]. Sending-Taking is a very effective practice for developing loving-kindness and compassion through the mindset of exchanging yourself for other. The practice of Sending and Taking" is also a type of shamatha practice, which is part of the main practice of insight into reality. Therefore, doing Sending and Taking not only serves to develop the motivation for the practice, bodhicitta, but also helps prepare you for the actual meditation on reality.

Sending and Taking is done over the coming and going of your breath. First, as you breathe in, you imagine that all of the unsatisfactorinesses, sufferings—sickness and pain, and so on—and mind obscurations of all sentient beings come into you in the form of a dark colour, like smoke. It enters your nostrils and dissolves into you. Think that all of the sufferings of all sentient beings have come to you. Then, as you breathe out, very pure, white light goes out from your nostrils and carries all of your happiness, merit, virtue accumulated from practising dharma, life energy, and goodness to all sentient beings. You think that it has gone to them. You do this for some time.

---

[28] Tib. gtong len.

Doing that will not make you sick or cause disturbances for you. To the contrary, your own life, merit, wisdom, and personal good qualities will increase, all of them. Why is that? The principal reason for your difficulties and suffering is self-cherishing. Whenever you hold onto self-cherishing, it always creates problems and suffering for you. When you do the practice of Sending and Taking, since it is the opposite of holding onto self-cherishing, its result is always the opposite of self-cherishing.

If you are successful in the practice, then, usually, at the end, the thought that you must attain buddhahood for the sake of sentient beings will arise, because that is the most effective method there could be for removing their sufferings and fulfilling their needs for happiness. If that kind of thought does arise, then you have aroused what is called fictional enlightenment mind.

Sometimes the enlightenment mind does not come automatically at the end of Sending and Taking practice, so you have deliberately to arouse it. How should this be done? On the basis of what you have developed so far, you could think, "I am one whereas other sentient beings are many. Of the two, one and many, which is most important? I am one person wanting happiness and not wanting suffering. All sentient beings are many; they are the most important. So, I will set every single sentient being, all the migrators of the six types, without one left out, at the level of a buddha". That mindset is the fictional enlightenment mind. There are other ways of thinking that end up with this same mind-set, too.

The fictional enlightenment mind is a very great mind, a very vast mind. To have it, you need the thought, "I myself will set every sentient being at the level of a buddha". Of course, whether you actually can do that or not is another question. However, it is the thought, "I will do it" that is important in this case.

These days, many people say, "Enlightenment mind is the thought to do something not just for myself but for all sentient beings". However, that is not enlightenment mind. It is the mind of the first two immeasurables—immeasurable loving-kindness and immeasurable compassion—but these alone are not enlightenment mind. Fictional enlightenment mind must have two reference points for it to be actual bodhicitta. The first is sentient beings; your mind must be considering all sentient beings without exception, not in a general way but specifically including every one of them. The second is buddhahood; your mind must be intent on setting every one of those sentient beings at the level of a fully, complete buddha. If your intent contains both of those, then it is fictional enlightenment mind.

Finally, there is the very important point that loving-kindness and compassion must be put together with emptiness. If you develop loving-kindness or compassion but it has a lot of self-grasping with it then, since everything is taken to be solid and true, it will only increase suffering. However, if your loving-kindness or compassion is joined with emptiness, then it can never increase suffering but will only ever increase the degree of loving-kindness and compassion. That is why the full instructions on development of enlightenment mind through Equalization and Exchange start with the development of superfactual enlightenment mind. In the actual instructions of Equalization and Exchange you are supposed to do a little bit of the development of superfactual enlightenment mind first so as to cut the solidification of self-grasping. That creates the true mental spaciousness needed for the practices of equalization and exchange followed by Sending and Taking to go easily and properly and to culminate in the development of fictional enlightenment mind.

To sum up, whatever meditation practice you do, to begin with you should always begin by taking refuge and follow that by arousing the thought, "The purpose for doing this meditation is so that every one of the sentient beings equivalent to space will attain the rank of a buddha".

The Main Practice

Development of Insight Into Reality Through the Practices of Shamatha and Vipashyana

The meditation on enlightenment mind sets the intention for the path we will follow; it ensures that our meditation goes in the right direction. The actual meditation of the path to enlightenment is the meditation that gets at the ground of our being, our inner reality, and makes it more and more manifest in our experience. There are many meditations that serve this purpose but in every Buddhist vehicle, from lowest to highest—including Great Completion and Mahamudra—all of them are summed up into two—shamatha and vipashyana.

In order to attain enlightenment, it is necessary to develop insight into reality. The Sanskrit name for this insight into reality is called vipashyana. The reality it sees is called "emptiness", meaning the absence of deluded realities, which in itself is reality. Now, vipashyana alone will not be effective at seeing emptiness; it needs to be steadied so that it can see the reality of emptiness clearly. Therefore, a technique is needed to provide the steadiness. The technique for that is the practice of making the mind abide calmly and that is called shamatha in Sanskrit, meaning "calm abiding".

Beginners usually have very wild, untamed minds. This kind of mind is not very useful if you want to do something with the mind. For this reason, although shamatha and vipashyana are needed together for the actual meditation on reality, when you start out on the path of meditation, it is usual to begin by doing shamatha practice alone. Shamatha practice is the practice of developing a mind that abides calmly, without disturbances, and abides stably, without effort. The calm and stable mind developed by shamatha practice is a workable frame of mind. It is suitable for doing any other kind of meditation, including vipashyana meditation, hence it is the basis of all other Buddhist meditations.

The traditional metaphor for the need for shamatha in relation to vipashyana goes like this. Mind can be likened to an oil lamp. An oil lamp has the quality of providing illumination; it dispels darkness. An oil lamp placed inside a dark room could illuminate the room and dispel the darkness. However, if there is a draught in the room, the lamp will not be able to do its job very well. Therefore, some protection needs to be provided so that the wind cannot blow the flame about. In the same way, mind has an illuminating quality that can bring brilliant knowing. However, the mind of an ordinary person has no control over itself and is blown about by external factors, therefore its innate illumination does not come out very strongly. If the mind is protected from that distraction, the illuminating quality of the mind can come on very strongly and bring brilliant knowing. The way to make the mind without distraction is to train it so that it can abide steadily and calmly wherever it is put. When the mind has been trained that way, the natural illuminating quality of the mind can be a spotlight that illuminates the reality of mind very clearly. The practice of training the mind to abide steadily and calmly is called "shamatha" or calm-abiding. The practice of insight that uses the illuminating quality of mind is called "vipashyana" or insight. Both practices are needed together because shamatha makes the mind both a steady and workable situation within which the vipashyana can function effectively to show the reality of the situation.

Different Ways of Meditating on Reality

There are two different approaches to the practices of shamatha and vipashyana corresponding to the way they are taught in the conventional or you could say exoteric teachings of the Buddha, called the sutra teachings, and how they are practised in the unconventional or you could say esoteric teachings of the Buddha, called the tantra teachings.

In the sutra teachings, there is a very graded approach. First you develop a good shamatha. That creates a workable situation of mind within which vipashyana can be developed. The vipashyana practice is taught as logical enquiry into the nature of reality. The vipashyana practice can be done separately from the shamatha practice but in the end, the two have to be put together.

In the tantra teachings, there are both graded and non-graded approaches. In the graded approaches found in the Mahamudra teachings, you practice shamatha first but this is done in a way that leads into the natural vipashyana of mind revealing itself. From that point on, the two are practised in union. In the ultimate approach of the Mahamudra and Great Completion teachings, there is no separate development of shamatha and vipashyana. Furthermore, vipashyana is not done as a logical enquiry that leads eventually to a direct perception of reality. Instead, your guru shows you the essence of your own mind, which is naturally-existing shamatha and vipashyana, already unified. This practice of shamatha and vipashyana does not rely on step-wise development of the practices and does not rely on logical examination of reality. Instead, you are shown the innate reality of your own mind and are shown how to rest within that directly.

The teachings here emphasise the sutra approach then give some instructions from the Mahamudra teachings and finally give a short introduction to the ultimate approach of Great Completion[29].

The Actual Practice of Meditation

The actual practice of meditation is taught by explaining the key points of the practices. In order to practice meditation, you need to learn and practice two sets of key points: the key points of the body; and the key points of the mind. These topics take up the remainder of the book. The key points of body is a straightforward discussion about how to position the body during meditation and takes up one chapter. The key points of mind are the instructions on how to use the mind to manifest your own internal reality, the ground of being or enlightened core discussed earlier. All of the key points of mind are summed up in the instructions of the two practices, shamatha and vipashyana. As before, these can be taught

---

[29] In other words, the teachings here show all the possibilities but they make the conventional approach of the sutras the most important point. This is because this book is about the most general level of teaching.

either according to the conventional instructions of the sutra path or the uncommon and special instructions of the tantra path.

The Main Practice

The Key Points of Body: Posture

Generally speaking, as our teacher the Buddha said, body and mind are like support and supported. Following on from that, you could say that body and mind are like a cup and the water contained in it. Now, if the cup is shaken around, the water will spill out all over the place, and likewise, if the body is not held well, the mind will not stay put. For this reason, the key points of the body are very important for beginners in meditation. Later, when you have done enough practice that the habitual patterns connected with the body have been purified, it is not essential to observe the key points of the body.

There are seven key points of body. 1) The legs are drawn up into crossed position, preferably into what is called vajra-asana. 2) The hands are placed in equipoise position, with the right palm on top of the left. Alternatively, the hands can be placed over the knees. 3) The shoulders are set evenly, in a posture like the wings of a vulture. There is no need to over-exert yourself at this. 4) This one is the most important: the spine should be straight like an arrow. 5) The chin and neck: the chin should be hooked in towards the neck just a little, it is said. The real issue here is that the upper part of the spine above the shoulders also is straight. If you set your head and neck so that the spine really is straight from bottom to top, you will find that there will be a natural, slight hooking of the chin in towards the neck and that is what is meant by this instruction. 6) The positioning of mouth and tongue: in general, the mouth and jaw should be relaxed. The mouth should not be closed but slightly open, with a slight space between the lips and teeth[30]. The tip of the tongue should be pressed gently to the upper palate. 7) The eyes and gaze: the gaze of the eyes can be placed downwards, straight ahead, or upwards. When looking downwards, the gaze is down a little. When looking upwards, the meaning is not that you have to stare forcefully into space or look up very high but that you gently look upwards a little. When you sit with one of these gazes for a long time, if it becomes tiresome, you can change to one of the other two. If you must close your eyes, you can, but it is not recommended. It is important to keep your eyes open while practising because, if you close them, the illuminating aspect of mind does not develop and, also, various thoughts and images will tend to appear in mind that would not otherwise appear and which you will tend to become caught up in. All in all, the eyes should be left open and looking ahead in a normal way.

These seven points come down to two most important ones: straight spine and relaxed body.

---

[30] In the Great Completion teachings it is additionally stated that the breath should pass through that gap, rather than through the nostrils. However, that is a very special technique and should not be used unless your teacher has instructed you in it.

THE MAIN PRACTICE

THE KEY POINT OF MIND: SHAMATHA

The practice of shamatha is the antidote to distraction. Doing the practice entails the development of two positive mental factors. The first is called "mindfulness" and the second is called "alertness". Mindfulness is the ability of mind to stay with its object. Alertness is the particular mental faculty that is alert to any straying from the object. If the mind strays, alertness informs the mind that there has been distraction allowing mindfulness to be re-asserted. Mindfulness is then re-asserted and the mind stays put on the object again.

Both mindfulness and alertness are needed in the development of shamatha. When the two are developed to the point that mind can, on demand, abide stably without any distraction at all, that is called equipoise and that kind of equipoise is the final goal of shamatha practice. It is the meditative state of mind which is needed as the basis for gaining insight.

There are two types of shamatha practice: with reference and without reference. Shamatha without reference is most commonly used in the Vajra Vehicle meditations of Mahamudra and Great Completion. In the more conventional practices of the sutra system, which are usually better for beginners, shamatha with reference is the way that shamatha is usually practised.

1. Shamatha Without Reference

In the higher meditations of Mahamudra and Great Completion, you just rest directly in the luminosity which is the nature of your own mind. This is a practice of shamatha and vipashyana unified together. The shamatha part is the resting directly without need of some object other than mind. The vipashyana part is that you are in the reality of your own mind, actually seeing the reality of your own mind. In this case, the style of shamatha is without reference. In the more conventional approaches to shamatha practice, you use some kind of object, such as a mental visualization, to keep the mind focussed one-pointedly; that is called shamatha with reference. In shamatha without reference, you do not use a special object as a way of keeping your mind focussed one-pointedly but just rest in the mind itself. In the higher meditations of Mahamudra and Great Completion, the staying one-pointedly in mind is called "non-distraction" and that you are simply staying in the luminosity which is the reality of your own mind, without creating anything, is called a "non-meditation" style of meditation.

This non-distracted and non-meditation style of meditation is actually very easy. It is the most easy thing to do because there is actually nothing to do. However, it is very difficult for most people to do that. Most people start thinking conceptually about the reality of their own mind in the middle of the meditation and thereby distract themselves from the reality they are trying to stay within. They keep on fiddling with what needs no adjustment and, because of that, make this practice of meditation which is actually exceptionally easy into something difficult. Therefore, for most people, it is better to start with a technique of meditation which is difficult! What is that? It is shamatha with reference!

2. Shamatha With Reference

What is the reference, that is, what is the object apart from itself that mind focusses on in the meditation? It can be many things. All sorts of different objects are explained as the basis for doing shamatha practice with reference. In this case, a practice of shamatha which is done using the objects of the six senses will be explained—the visual forms that appear to the eye; the sounds of the ear; the smells of the nose; the tastes of the tongue; the contacts of touch of the body; and all phenomena which are the objects of mind.

Normally, the objects of the six senses cause distraction; because of them, the afflictions arise, and because of them, confusion occurs. If there were no object of the senses then the perceiver of them, the subject[31], would not happen, would it?

When you become distracted in meditation, it is these six objects that are the principal cause of the distraction. If you were to turn them into meditation, then they would be part of the meditation and hence would cease to be problematic. For example, if you have an enemy, it means that there is someone who will harm you, so you need a tough bodyguard to protect

---

[31] If there were no perceived objects, then there would be no perceiving mind of them; such a mind would just cease. In other words, if the apparently outer objects were removed then the dualistic consciousnesses relating to them would cease, too. This is a key point of the Kagyu presentation of meditation.

you, and there will be fighting back and forth because of it. That is a difficult situation, isn't it? However, if that enemy is turned into a friend, you will not have an enemy so there will be no need for a tough assistant, and no need to fight. In the same way, if you turn the six objects of the senses into assistants of your meditation, you will not need defences against them and they will no longer harm you.

Well then, how are the six objects turned into assistants of meditation? There are many methods for doing so; it can be done through shamatha meditation, loving-kindness and compassion meditation, emptiness meditation, essence of mind meditation, and so on. Here, the shamatha way of approaching them is explained.

What is the essence of shamatha? It is mindfulness. You can say that, if there is mindfulness, there is shamatha and if not, there is not shamatha. That is the way to make the distinction between shamatha being present or not; whether there are discursive thoughts or not is not used to make the distinction of whether there is shamatha or not. Thus, mindfulness is the principal thing in shamatha practice. If there is mindfulness, all sense objects will be turned into meditation.

If mindfulness turns sense objects into meditation, then it means that mindfulness turns the sense objects from being the enemy that causes distraction and harm to shamatha into their opposite, an assistant of shamatha. How are objects turned into the assistant of shamatha? The answer is that mindfulness must be brought to the six sense objects and put together with them.

Mindfulness then is the principal cause or means by which the natural potential or innate qualities of your own mind are brought forth. At the moment, the natural potential or innate qualities of your mind are not fully evident. The principal means for bringing them forth is mindfulness. To make an example of this: the human body has a great deal of natural potential but the potential will not be brought out unless the body is exercised and trained. You can use some temporary means to relieve problems with the body such as taking medicine but these usually bring other problems, for example, taking heart medicine might cause incidental problems with the lungs. However, if you train the body well, it will not only cure these kinds of problems but will prevent them from coming in the future. Likewise, if you develop mindfulness, it can only improve your mind in this life and, ultimately, it does lead to enlightenment. As with the body, you could use some temporary means to solve the various passing problems of mind, for example, you could go dancing to cheer yourself up, but these don't really solve anything except in a very temporary way. Mindfulness is the root by which the natural potential, the innate qualities of mind, can be brought forth and ultimately manifested as complete enlightenment.

One way to train mindfulness is to use the six sense objects as a basis for its development. This kind of practice is shamatha practice with a reference; the reference is the six sense objects.

1. Mindfulness of Visual Forms

What is the object of the eye? The eye experiences two things: visual forms and colours. It does not hear sounds, smell smells, taste tastes, and so on. Correspondingly, the sense object of the eye—visual form or colour—is only ever perceived by the eye seeing it. When the eye sees its sense objects and, together with that, the mind also knows that, that is, is mindful of it, then the visual form and colour seen by the eye have become a support of meditation. Therefore, it is necessary that the eye sees its object and together with that, that the mind also sees it. For example, if you were to look at your own hand for one hour and if there was nothing intervening between your eye and your hand, then your eye would be seeing your hand for that hour. However, it is very unlikely that your mind would also be seeing your hand for that hour. During those moments when the mind was also seeing the hand, that is precisely when there is also mindfulness with mind. At the other times mind is somewhere else and there is no mindfulness of the visual sense object.

To meditate using the visual forms as a support for meditation, it is good to place a small object, for example a flower, before you and look at that. When you look at the flower, the mind will initially stay with the flower then, after that, it will go off somewhere else. When it wanders away and you notice that it has wandered, look at the flower with your eyes and mind again. If you do that repeatedly, the mind will become more tranquil, it will be tamed, and the discursive thoughts and afflictions will be alleviated. Longchen Rabjam said about this in his *Trilogy on Resting Up in Absorption*,

> Abiding on the support of a reference
> Non-reference is fully produced;
> By relying on a reference
> It becomes possible to produce non-reference.

The meaning is that by having a reference, that is, by relying on a reference, the mind is tamed. When the mind becomes tamed, discursive thoughts are naturally alleviated.

Generally speaking, for the whole time that we have been circling in samsaric existence, from beginningless time until now, mind has always worked in a dualistic process of perceived object and perceiving subject. At this point in time, we are using the perceived object to develop mindfulness and that will later assist the transcendence of the perceived object and hence of the perceiver, too. Why is that? From time without beginning up to the present our mind has worked with both objects known by consciousness and their subjective consciousnesses. Moreover, mind involved with that subject-object way of knowing has had no control over itself. Meditation is a way to deal with this sort of mind which is out of control and, of the two sides of this type of mind—object and subject, it is easiest to start with meditation that works with the object. We start by using the objects of consciousness to develop mindfulness. From that beginning we can go all the way through to abandoning the dualistic type of mind.

A. To do this kind of meditation, first relax your mind. Then, look continuously at a visual form. When you do this practice, the eyes will usually become uncomfortable. In addition to that, three other things can happen. First, the eyes can go out of focus and two images of the object can be seen. Second, the object can become darkened and indistinct. Third, the object can move around in the visual field. These are not faults. It is normal for the eyes to hurt, of course; we do not usually stare at one thing for a long time and if we do, the eyes start to hurt. Then, you might see double but as long as your mind is with that, that is, as long as there is mindfulness with it, it is all right. Then, if the object becomes dark and or indistinct, again, as long as your mind is staying there with it, it is all right.

B. Now for a second approach to this meditation. In the first approach, you used a specific visual object as the basis for doing the meditation. In this second approach, you do not use a specific visual object, rather, you let any visual object that appears to your visual sense become the basis of the meditation. To do this, start by relaxing your mind. Then stay with whatever the eye sees. Again, as before, when you do this, there is no need to think about anything. When doing this, there could be times when you do not notice a particular visual object but that doesn't matter; in those cases, if you can keep your mindfulness with that, the meditation continues on and the natural relaxation of mind will still appear.

While doing these practices involving looking with the eye, the eyes can start to hurt. If that happens, you can stay with the painful sensations instead of the visual objects. If you do that, it changes to meditation on the fifth of the six sense objects, the sensations of the body.

When you do this second type of practice, if you can stay with one object that appears to the visual sense, then that is good but usually you won't be able to stay with any one object for very long. The mind tends to behave like a frog; it stays on one visual form for a while then it jumps to another where it stays for a while before jumping to another, and so on. However, as long as your mindfulness is staying with it, wherever it goes, it is fine. If you can do that, then the basis of the meditation is occurring nicely and because of that the meditation will also turn out well.

This kind of meditation in which the mind is brought together with an object of the senses is useful for everyone who has not yet overcome the distraction of mind. For those who have already started to meditate, it can be a useful technique for improving the quality of the meditation that they have already developed. For those who have already developed sufficient skill at meditation that they have little or no distraction, it is not used.

2. Mindfulness of Sounds

With visual forms, the mind is connected with whatever visual form is seen by the eye whereby the visual form becomes a support for the development of non-distraction. Similarly here, the ear listens to sounds and mind is connected with whatever sounds are heard. If there are many different sounds, it is not necessary to keep the mind with just one of them; just connect mind with whatever sounds are heard and that will be sufficient. To do this, as before, first sit with a relaxed mind. Then, listen to sounds. If you try too hard, this will not work; you will be trying so hard to hear the sounds that you will not be able to do the practice. If that happens, try *not* listening to sounds deliberately and that will usually work. The actual instruction is to listen to sounds but for people who are too tight, the instruction can be changed to "not listen", meaning that these people should just sit there and let the sounds come to them, without deliberately trying to listen.

If you do the two practices discussed so far, any and every visual form and colour and any and every sound can be turned into an assistant of meditation. Compare this with the person who thinks that he will meditate to get peace and quiet for himself but who does not know the actual techniques or meaning of meditation. For that kind of person, meditation is a retreat from his world and that, ultimately speaking, cannot work. For them, any sound or visual movement becomes a disturbance that stops their meditation. On the other hand, for the person who practises the meditation discussed here, these things become aids to the meditation.

3. Mindfulness of Smells

If you understand how to do the meditation with sights and sounds, then the meditation with smells will be easy. For this, whatever smell comes to the nose is used. It can be pleasant, unpleasant, a single smell or many smells mixed but whatever it is, the mind must be put together with that sensation of smell.

4. Mindfulness of Tastes

The next step is the connection of mind to tastes. This again, is the same sort of thing. Whatever taste there is—pleasant, unpleasant, acidic, bitter, and so on—just that is used as the basis of the meditation.

5. Mindfulness of Touch

The next step is the connection of mind to bodily sensations or contacts as they are called. Again, whatever sensation appears to the body is used as the basis of the meditation; it can be roughness, smoothness, weightiness, cold, heat, a pain in the back, a pain in the head, a pain in the knees, and so on.

Because the sensations become useful in terms of developing mindfulness, every one of them, whether normally seen as good and bad, painful or otherwise, is actually good. For example, if you have a tooth-ache, you cannot keep your attention away from it, the mind is always with it. You can try to divert yourself from the pain by some means such as watching a movie or going for a walk in a nice garden but your mind will just keep coming back to the pain. Now the thought,

"I've got an ache", actually assists the toothache and makes it more solid, likewise the thought, "I'm sick", and so on, actually helps to solidify whatever sickness you might have. And the follow-up thoughts such as, "This ache (or sickness or whatever) is no good", only serve to intensify the pain or feeling of sickness further. They are like wind that fans a fire and makes it blaze. Moreover, the more of them there are, the worse it gets, just like the stronger the wind, the more the fire blazes. So, these trains of thoughts such as, "I'm sick. This illness is no good. It is harming me. When will this illness be cured?", and so on are the principal assistants to the actual sickness.

Rather than allowing these kinds of thoughts to follow on from the pains and aches of illness, discomfort, etcetera, the pains and aches themselves should have mind connected to them. When you do have pain or discomfort, just look right at the pain or discomfort; bring your attention to it. By doing that, it will be turned into an aid of meditation as already described for the sensations of eye, and so forth.

In addition to that, since these kinds of thoughts only create more problems, you can take a different approach to illness and discomfort; you can talk to yourself like this: "If I'm sick, I'm sick", and "I will take medicine and, if it helps, it helps". Then, if taking medicine doesn't help, leave it at that, thinking, "The medicine didn't help. I did what I could and that's all there is to it. There's nothing else to be done. All right, no need to agonize over it any further."

6. Mindfulness of Mind

The final possibility is connection of mind to the contents of mind. Anything that occurs in the mind at all can be an object of the meditation. For example, following on from the above discussion of illness or painful problems, mind tends to keep coming back to the feelings of pain. Because of that, if you put your mind with the painful feelings, it becomes a very good way to increase mindfulness. And not only that but the extra thoughts about the discomfort or illness such as, "This pain is no good, it is bad", etcetera, will disappear. The painful sensation of body might stay and the unpleasant feelings connected with that in mind also might stay—though in some cases one or both can disappear, too—but the extra, anguish-producing thoughts are removed. When these kinds of thoughts have been removed, it is even possible to be happy despite the physical sensation of pain. In fact, since our basic nature is ease and joy, it is possible for that kind of very deep joy to come together with the physical pain once the mental hand-wringing has been removed. So, if you do have an ache or other discomfort, relax your mind and look at the physical sensations involved and the mental feelings associated with it, and keep your mindfulness together with that.

Summary of the Development of Mindfulness Through the Six Sense Objects

Which of the six sense objects is best for doing this practice? Any and all of them are useful. For any one person, whichever sense object is clear at any given time can be used for the practice. For some people, sights are easiest, for some sounds, and so on. Use whichever of them you find is easiest.

Say you are listening to sounds. You have a pain. You think to yourself, "I am listening to sounds. The pain is no good. I must not look at the pain. I must listen to sounds". However, that will cause your attention to become more focussed on the pain and you might think, "This pain is disrupting my meditation". If that happens, you have not understood the key points of this type of meditation. If you do understand them, then you will understand that everything can be turned into an aid to meditation. The key point here is that distraction itself is the means by which mindfulness is developed. Thus distraction is all right as long as it becomes the cause of mindfulness. If you understand this well, then everything can be turned into an aid to meditation. And then, no matter where you are, you can always be happy. And you will not have anything that arises as an obstacle, instead, everything will arise as an assistant and everything will be seen as an embellishment of enjoyment. And you will have a truly expansive mind.

For example, you are meditating and hear a sound. If you think, "This sound is no good", and because of that decide that you cannot meditate any further, then that is a sign that you have not understood the key points of this meditation. On the other hand, if you do understand the technique here, then that sound can become an aid to your meditation. If you use it as such, the sounds will be heard more and more clearly. Therefore, when sounds do occur in your meditation, you can connect your mind with them and then, no matter how much sound there is, it does not matter. If there are one hundred thousand sounds then there are also one hundred thousand aids to your meditation. Thus, when you are sitting in meditation and do hear sounds, you do not need to think, "This sound is disturbing my meditation". If you do think that way, then you have not understood the key point of meditation and then, no matter where you are, your meditation can always be harmed by sound. For example, you are meditating in a big city with its many noises of cars, taxis, construction work, and so on. You don't know to use the sound as part of your practice and drive yourself crazy thinking that the sound is disturbing your meditation. Thinking that this is not a place for meditation, you go to an isolated place in the mountains. But, once you get there, you find that there are all sorts of other noises: the sound of small animals, the sound of the wind, and the trees, and so on. So you decide that that also is not a good place for meditation and move elsewhere. This kind of behaviour shows why the Buddha said that mind is like a monkey. Monkeys cannot sit still and because of it, they create trouble un-necessarily. Where there is no trouble, they create trouble. Moreover, the trouble they create at first is small but if left unattended it gets worse. Mind likewise makes trouble where there is none. At first it makes a small problem but then because it clings and ties itself in knots, it makes more and more trouble. Thus, all the worry that can come because of not understanding the key points of meditation are just meaningless. This is just each person making their own problems for themselves. At the same time, these troubles are all just fictions created by mind; they come because of grasping and the wound up state that happens because of it.

3. The Steps In the Development Of Shamatha

If you do practise shamatha meditation, your mind will gradually abide more and more. In the instructions on Mahamudra, the improvement of the ability to abide is taught in three, successively-more-stable levels of abiding, as follows. The first level is called "Abiding like a cataract crashing down the face of a mountain". At very first when you practise meditation, you do not notice anything much in mind; it seems as though nothing is happening. However, after you have practised for a little while, you start to notice that you have enormous amounts of discursive thought crashing about all over the place and it seems, as you continue to practise, that the amount of discursive thought is only increasing. In fact, the discursive thoughts are not increasing, it is just that you are now noticing them because your meditation has increased the illuminating property of mind. For example, if you look at a river which is full of fish but which is also highly polluted, you do not see the fish. However, if the river is cleaned up, then you start to see more and more fish as the level of pollution decreases. The fish have not changed in number at all but the clearness of the water has allowed the fish that are there to become increasingly visible. At this point, if you think to yourself, "This discursive thought is no good", and attempt to stop it, the discursive thought will only get worse and worse and the natural quality of relaxation will not come forth. So, there is no need to worry over this discursive thought that has been discovered. Instead, if you continue to meditate, you will begin to notice that sometimes you are distracted and sometimes not and you will begin to know the difference between distraction and non-distraction. If you continue, the non-distraction will become stronger and stronger. As you continue your practice, you will pass through the middling and final stages of abiding, which are called "abiding like a gently flowing river" and "abiding like an ocean" respectively. In the second stage, there are both distraction and non-distraction though the latter has become strong. In the final stage, discursive thoughts either do not arise or, if they do, they immediately return to the ocean without affecting the abiding at all. At this point there is on-going non-distraction[32].

4. Rough and Smooth Experiences Along the Way

Meditating like that will cause various experiences to arise. Overall, the various experiences that occur to a meditator are ones that seem either in or out of harmony with meditation.

---

[32] In other words, a perfect shamatha has been developed.

The former are called "smooth experiences" and the latter "rough experiences" of meditation.

The smooth experiences are the experiences that will seem as though they are important to meditation or are the actual goals of meditation. Because of this, it is easy to take them as final and be side-tracked by them even though they are only temporary experiences which are not final. All the different varieties of these temporary experiences can be summed up into three basic types: bliss, illumination, and no-thought. The bliss experience is that body or mind or both become very light and easy and filled with pleasant feelings. When this experience comes very strongly, all that appears in one's experience is seen as blissful. The illumination experience is that everything seems exceptionally clear to the mind. The no-thought experience is that all discursive thought stops for a while and there is a very empty feeling with it. These three can and do come by themselves and they can and do come in combination, two or even three at a time. Sometimes they come very strongly and sometimes only weakly. If two come together, one can be strong and the other weak, both can be strong, or both can be weak, and so on. They come as a result of meditation but there is nothing fixed about when they come or not. Sometimes one will come, sometimes another. The key point is that these are only temporary experiences so they are not goals in and of themselves. If you take them as important and cling to them, they will become an obstacle to the further development of your meditation. Therefore the instruction connected with them is,

> Do not reject them on the one hand and do not cling to them on the other.

The rough experiences are the various experiences in and out of actual meditation that seem inimical to meditation. In terms of a session of meditation, the rough experiences are summed up in the two types of experience: sinking and agitation. "Sinking" refers to the situation where mind sinks down and becomes dull. It includes mind becoming listless and disinterested; it goes to sleep or, even if it doesn't go to sleep, it closes in and becomes very thick. Sinking occurs because the illuminating factor of mind decreases so sinking is also said to be the absence of that factor. "Agitation" is when discursive thought appears in mind. This ranges from a single, very subtle thought popping up and subtly disturbing the meditation to very strong thoughts running so wild that mind is all over the place and it is impossible to tell whether you are meditating or not.

All of those types of temporary experience, both the smooth and rough ones, come to meditators. Both of them are good in the sense that they are signs of meditation; they are signs that appear because meditation is being done. If you put them on a scale, you would find that they are the same; both of them are good. The rough ones are not pleasant, so there is a tendency to regard them as bad and the smooth ones are pleasant so there is a tendency to regard them as good. However, both of them are helpful to meditation. Therefore, there is a way to approach them: do not cling to the smooth experiences and do not be averse to the rough experiences.

THE MAIN PRACTICE

THE KEY POINT OF MIND: VIPAŚHYANĀ THE TWO TRUTHS AND EMPTINESS

The Buddha Bhagavat's whole teaching of dharma has two aspects to it, which are called in Sanskrit, upaya and prajna, and in English, method and intelligence. The various practices discussed so far are methods that support the application of intelligence or prajna to the investigation of reality. Now, we turn to the explanations of insight in which the mind's intelligence or prajna is used to investigate reality.

1. What is Prajna?

Prajna is the critical faculty of mind that can determine that something is this or that in a very exacting kind of way. The word itself means "a better kind of knower", one that knows the real situation, the situation as it is. It is the kind of mind that can be used to know the truth of any given situation. In the Buddhist tradition, prajna is specifically used to end delusion that prevents the true situation being known. There are various levels of delusion which go all the way down to the fundamental ignorance of thinking that people and phenomena truly exist. Each level of delusion produces a mistake in the way that the world is perceived. In Buddhism, prajna is used to investigate all these levels of deluded reality and find the actual situation, the actual reality.

2. Two Levels of Reality

The Buddha pointed out that what we think of as mind is a fairly complex process and one which is fundamentally mistaken. It comes about because of a fundamental type of ignorance. This "ignorance", as it is called, takes all things and beings as real. It ignores, and so does not see, the actual situation, which is that all things and beings are not real. Once this kind of ignorance has set in, the mind that results sees everything in terms of this and that solidified thing. It is a dualistic kind of mind. Another name for dualistic mind is rational mind. It gets this name because it sees and knows and considers everything in terms of this and that. This term rational mind is very important. It refers to the mind that produces all of the mistakes and maintains all of the dualities after the fundamental ignorance has occurred.

Dualistic mind does not correctly comprehend the actuality of its object, what it is observing. Instead of seeing it as it is, it apprehends it as solidly real. This process of apprehending a solid reality in things is called "grasping at truth in things". Here, truth does not mean the truth which is the actual situation but a kind of existence which is solidified and seems to be really and truly there, even though it is not.

Thus, beings who are under the sway of fundamental ignorance are not seeing the actual situation. What they are seeing is a fictional situation made up by the ignorance and rationalizing that goes with it. However, they believe in that reality, so it is "true" for them. Thus, the reality that all beings under the sway of ignorance create and live in is called "fictional truth". At the same time as they are seeing their fictional truth, there is an actual situation going on which they are not seeing. If the fundamental ignorance is removed, this actual situation will be seen. Buddhas and other beings who have progressed on the path to the point of having removed the fundamental ignorance do see this actual situation. This actual situation is a superior reality that is a fact and which is seen as true by the spiritually advanced beings that do see it. Therefore, the Buddha called it "superfactual truth".

Prajna can be applied to the fictional level of reality in two different ways. In one way, you just look at the things that are conceived of in that reality to see whether your concept of them is correct or not. If you look with correct prajna, that is, if the reasoning you use is correct, you might discover that you were making a mistake about them. For example, if you look at how rational mind conceives of things, you find that it takes them to be permanent. However, if you look into them, you find that they are impermanent. In this case, you have not corrected the fundamental ignorance of taking them to be truly existent but you have at least corrected your view of them within fictional truth.

In a second way, you could look more closely at the things of the fictional reality to see whether they do truly exist. If you look with correct prajna, you discover that all the phenomena and beings, including yourself, that ignorance has apprehended as true are, in fact, not really there. You have come to the actual situation of all phenomena, which is that they are empty, devoid of these objects that have been trumped up on the basis of ignorance. Thus, their absence in fact is called their emptiness, or just "emptiness". This is the superfactual truth.

Thus, prajna can be the antidote to delusion at all levels. Most especially though, a specific kind of prajna can be used to undo the fundamental ignorance of dualistic mind. Anyone who develops that kind of prajna can thus escape from the mistaken dualistic world that they have created and return to their original, innate and factual reality, which is buddhahood.

When prajna is practically applied so that insight into the actual situation, whether it is at the level of fictional truth or superfactual truth is obtained, that is called vipashyana, "insight". It is the insight of vipashyana, joined to the stability of shamatha that allows a practitioner of meditation to see the actual situation.

In Buddhist meditation, shamatha and vipashyana are put together in order to see the actual situation. The shamatha provides the stability of mind and the vipashyana provides the insight to see the situation clearly. The unsatisfactoriness of beings is a direct result of fundamental ignorance. That ignorance and its attendant unsatisfactoriness can be dispelled by meditation in which shamatha is unified with the type of prajna that looks to find the actual situation at the superfactual level.

3. How to Develop Prajna

The Buddha taught his disciples in a gradual way. He did not try to teach them the prajna that eliminates all the things that exist first because it would have been too overwhelming for many of them. Instead, he showed them the prajna that corrects the view of existent things first then, later, when they had removed some of their delusion and were more open, he showed them the prajna that leads to the insight that those existent things do not exist. The teachings on vipashyana in this book follow the same sequence. In essence, the Lesser Vehicle approach is shown first, then the sutra Great Vehicle approach is shown.

4. Prajna Examines the Fictional Truth: Three Mis-apprehensions

According to the lowest of the four schools of Buddhist philosophy, the Vaibhashika or Particularist school, things are either external, physical things or internal mind. This is a convenient way to sum up all of the things which we, because of our fundamental ignorance, regard as existent. Rational mind apprehends all of these existent things in wrong ways. The Buddha taught these: 1) it apprehends permanence in things where there is really impermanence; 2) it apprehends singularity in things where there is really multiplicity; and 3) it apprehends independence in things where there is really dependence.

These three wrong perceptions will be found in mind with every problem you experience. Thus, overcoming them is a major step towards reducing unsatisfactoriness. Moreover, they are symptoms of the fundamental ignorance that takes phenomena to be really, truly existing. Thus, overcoming them is a step towards dealing with that fundamental ignorance.

1. Permanence

One of the facets of fictional truth is that all phenomena are impermanent in nature. All of them change from moment to moment. Thus, all such things are impermanent, aren't they? Despite that, if you look, you will see that your rational mind apprehends things as permanent.

When rational mind apprehends permanence in its objects, it sees things as permanent, as fixed and unchanging. Take a glass for example. If you put a glass on a table then read on for a little, then think about the glass again: is the glass that you are looking at now the same as the one you originally put on the table or is it different? A glass is changing from moment to moment. Thus, the glass that was there to begin with is not there now. That original glass has finished. The glass that has continued on from it is present now. It is not the same glass as the original but is a continuation of it. That is the case but our rational minds think that it is the same glass as before. Why? Because it has the same shape, colour, size, and so on as the glass that you knew before. Because of its similarity to something else that you knew earlier, rational mind categorizes it as that earlier thing. This is rational mind apprehending permanence in something that is in fact impermanent. A similar example is that we talk of ourselves when we were younger and now at the present time, and think of the two as being the same. That also is apprehending permanence where there is impermanence. Our dualistic, rational minds mistakenly perceive all things like that. Mind is fooled by the appearances, like watching a rapidly spinning fan yet thinking that the axis of the fan is stationary.

All compounded things are impermanent. At first they do not exist and then, because they are produced, they come into existence. Thus, they have a connection with time. Now, what is time? Time is comprised of past, present, and future. Of these, the past is finished and the future has not come about. Thus past and future do not exist. Any object connected with time must likewise exist only in the present time. Take three years: the past year, the present year, and the coming year. The past year has finished. The coming year has not happened. Thus there is only the present year. Now, it is, say, the seventh month. The sixth month has finished and the eighth not come. Then it is, say, the eleventh day. The tenth day is finished and the twelfth not come. Then it is, say, eleven o'clock. Ten has finished and twelve has not come. Then it is, say, twenty-four minutes past the hour. Within this minute, the seconds are passing one by one and within those seconds, the instants are here, now, now, now, as you snap your fingers. There is only this present, instant by instant. We think that things exist. If they do, they could only exist in the present moment, instant by instant. In other words, things are impermanent.

All the things we take to exist do change like this, instant by instant. Your body changes like that; the furniture around you changes like that; the house that you are sitting in changes like that; all of the worlds in all of the universes change like that. If they didn't change, they wouldn't be able to be. The process of cause, conditions, and their results would not happen, could not happen.

You have three thousand sheets of paper in a pile. Your rational mind takes the pile of paper to be a permanent thing. You take a large hammer and drive a spike right through the stack. The spike penetrates the first, second, and so on sheets, each in a fraction of an instant. The moments involved are very, very short. Yet, at any given moment, it is penetrating whatever it is penetrating. Everything before that has gone and ceased; everything that will come after it has yet to happen. It is a very rapid sequence of change in the present moment and the pile of paper exists only in each of those present moments. The pile of paper is impermanent.

The very rapid, instant by instant, level of impermanence is called "subtle impermanence" in our Buddhist tradition. There is also the "coarse impermanence" which is that some things change slowly enough that we do not notice the change as they are changing. However, if you look more closely, you will see that those things also are changing from moment to moment. You do not get old all of a sudden, do you? In a similar way, all of the worlds, in all of the universes are also aging, even though it is not immediately obvious. Thus all things do change from moment to moment, whether the change is obvious or not.

Understanding impermanence can be very beneficial. If you understand impermanence, your mind will tend not to become small and tight. When you do not understand impermanence, it is very easy to get upset over small things. Something that does not go quite right makes you think, "This is not all right, this is really a problem, I need this the way that I want it to be. I must have it the way I want. If I don't get what I want, it's not all right!" Then you really get yourself caught up over that small thing. On the other hand, if you understand emptiness, you will understand that things do not always work out the way you might want; realistically speaking, that is how it is. Some things will work out, some not, that is the nature of things! Because of that, you cannot always have things turn out the way you want. Of course, it is also not true that everything always cannot turn out the way you want. When you understand impermanence, you can just accept things as they are at any given moment.

For example, this understanding can help you to do your best at any given time. Whether it is your work, your meditation, your livelihood, some worldly work, or some dharma work, just do it to the best of your ability and then don't have any further expectation about it. "I will do my best then maybe it can work out well, perhaps not. After all, everything is impermanent, isn't it?" If you think that way, you will strike a balance and your mind will remain easy. Funnily enough, because of that, you will be able to do more work, more study, more meditation. Having a sense of perspective is very important. A sense of perspective comes from understanding reality and impermanence is one aspect of reality.

Previously in America, a man purchased a lottery ticket. He was an old man and developed an illness that took him to hospital. He was in the hospital when the lottery was drawn, so, although he won the lottery of over one hundred million dollars, he did not hear about it. His wife and children did hear about it and were very excited about the prospect of telling him the really good news. They went down to the hospital but, when they met the old man's doctor, the doctor advised them that it would be better not to tell the old man, because the excitement could kill him. The family discussed it at length and decided in the end that they should tell the father the news. However, they asked the doctor if he would do this to minimize the chance of over-exciting the father. The doctor agreed and went to see the old man. The doctor wove around the subject, very slowly introducing the possibility that the old man might have won a lot of money. The old man told the doctor that it didn't matter much to him whether he won the money or not and in fact, if he did win, he would give half of it to the doctor. The doctor joked with him, saying that he didn't mean it. The old man said, "No, no, it's really true; I'll give you half if I win". He was very calm about it. So the doctor said, "Would you put that in writing?" The old man said, "If you bring me a pen, I'll do it now". The doctor provided pen and paper and the old man made the declaration and put his signature to it. The doctor, on taking the paper, was so overwhelmed at the realization that he had just obtained over fifty million dollars that he had a heart attack and died. The old man was amazed, and wondered why the doctor had died all of a sudden. Later, the old man's wife and children arrived and told him of his win. At that point, he understood why the doctor had died—it was because of his great attachment and grasping to himself. The old man went home a few days later. His relative lack of attachment and grasping to the money that he had won had kept him safe from a major problem and also allowed him to enjoy his prize.

The stock market provides another example. As you probably know, the stock market goes up and down. When it goes down, you lose money, and sometimes it can be a lot of money. If you have money in the stock market and you watch the market going up and down with a very tight mind, then you can really have a lot of worry. But, honestly speaking, where is the value in this? If all of the worry and suffering that people generate for themselves when the stock market goes down could actually reverse the down trend, if it could even make the market go back up by one cent, then you could say there was some value to the worry and suffering. However, it cannot! The worry and suffering is just what it is, neither good nor bad, but it definitely doesn't have any value, any usefulness to it! If people who engage in the stock market knew about impermanence, if they had some sense of reality, then it would really help them a lot. They would know that sometimes the market goes up and sometimes down, that it does not always go where they might want it to go. Do what you can do, do the best you can, make your efforts, then accept things as they land.

Having a light touch is important with everything. When you drink a glass of water, you could do it the hard way, with a very tight mind, or you could relax, pick up the glass, and drink from it. If you do the former, there is a chance that you will drop the glass, or swallow the wrong way; something can go wrong. But, if you just pick it up gently and drink from it easily then you do what you need to do and that's it.

Generally speaking, whenever there is a problem you should stop and look carefully to see if there is a solution. If there is, then that is it. If not, then just accept it without worrying further or letting your mind get upset over it. After all, if there is no solution, further worry is not going to help at all. As in the example above, worrying about the stock market cannot change it and so is of no benefit. Thus, at all times leave your mind spacious and vast, but do what you can and do not follow it up by worrying about it. That is important.

2. Singularity

When you say "I", do you think one thing or many things? Likewise with things other than yourself; when you cognize them, does your mind take them as one thing or many things? For us, the mind puts "I" together with the concept of singularity, not multiplicity. And likewise, when it cognizes other things, it apprehends them as entities that are a single thing, not entities that are made up of a number of parts. This process is called "apprehending singularity". You do this with everything that your rational mind perceives; if it is a table you are looking at, then, despite the fact that it is made of legs, a top, and other parts, you see it as "one". When you think of yourself, despite the fact that you are made of many parts—arms, legs, organs, and so on—you see yourself as "one".

These things all are a multiplicity yet your rational mind mistakenly views them as singularities.

3. Independence

Is your hand itself you or not? How do you talk about yourself? You say, "I am not this part of my body, not that part of my body, not the abdomen, not the arm, not the mind, etcetera. I am not my hand, not my arm, not my leg, and so on". Your mind, when it says "I", takes it as something independent from the rest of body and mind, something that does not come in dependence on the body and mind, which is a mistake. This is called "the apprehension of independence". The reality of compounded phenomena is that they are dependent, not independent as seen by rational mind.

2. Prajna Examines for Superfactual Truth: Emptiness

In the last step, we used prajna to analyse the things that make up our worlds. By applying prajna, we found out that we were mistaken about how those things are situated at the fictional level and corrected some major mistakes. However, we still think that those things really do exist. The next step is to use prajna to look more closely at those things and see whether they really do exist or not. If we analyse the existence of those things, then we will find that those things are devoid, or empty as it is called, of the true existence that ignorance apprehends in them. This absence of true existence that we normally think is there is called "emptiness".

What does the word "emptiness" mean? It is composed of two parts. "Empty" refers to the absence of true existence described at the beginning of this chapter. The "ness" part is explained in various ways, according to the level of the teaching being given. One way of explaining "ness" is that it means that the empty aspect is totipotent, that is, that all things can come from it. All together, the word "emptiness" should be understood to mean that anything that appears is at the same time empty of true existence and anything that is empty at the same time will appear. In other words, emptiness should be taken to mean that phenomena exist as paired appearance and emptiness.

What is it that is empty? All dharmas, meaning all phenomena, are not truly existent. Well, then what constitutes dharmas? As suggested earlier, one way to look at it is to say that it includes all external, physical things and all internal, minds. Physical things are made up of matter, which is made of atoms. Minds are made up of moments of consciousness. Thus, to look into phenomena and how they exist, we have to investigate atomic matter on the one hand and time on the other. Of the two, we will investigate time, first.

Time is made up of past, present, and future, isn't it? We leave aside the past and present because the past has ceased and the future has not yet arrived. Now, this thing called the present, what is that? It is that which has come about and not yet ceased. Thus, if we are to find the present, we need to find something that has come about and not yet ceased. Let us look for that. In the example of the three thousand sheets of paper that are penetrated in a moment by a spike driven through them by a large hammer, there are three thousand very minute moments of time. Let us say that one of those moments is the present moment. What went before it is the past moment and what will succeed it will be the future moment. Is there a connection or not between the present and its past moment or the present moment and its future moment we have just isolated? If there were no connection, then the present moment could not arise on the basis of the past moment and the future moment could not arise on the basis of the present moment, either. There must be a connection but, if there is, the present is not the present moment but the present plus the past or future. Therefore, the actual present moment is less than and has to be taken out from that. If you continue this investigation, the present moment just cannot be found. If you investigate again and again, you will never find the thing called time that your rational, dualistic mind presents to you. You will see that there is no present and that, there being no present, there is no past and no future, either.

In a similar way, you can investigate matter and see that it also does not exist. If you look into atomic matter, you find that atoms also have parts and that those sub-atomic particles are also made of parts or energy. You just cannot find an atom the way that rational mind believes it to be there, as a self-existing entity.

Western scientists have some understanding of how the world that appears to us is very much a matter of a world projected by our concepts and is not there except for our concepts. For example, in science, there is the principle that no experiment is independent of the observer. When the observer sets up the experiment, the experiment itself changes. This shows that the world around us is not a solid, fixed entity the way our rational mind perceives it but a fluid, interdependent reality.

Thus, there is no solid time, there are no solid atoms and no solid worlds in solid universes. The chairs and furniture around you are not there the way your rational, dualistic mind sees them. The tea you drink likewise is not really there.

They are not there the way that your rational mind tells you that they are yet they still function; you can still drink a cup of tea and it will quench your thirst and might even be tasty.

Well, despite what you have just found, there is time, isn't there? If you asked someone about it, what would they say? They would say there is time! And what is it? They would say, there is lots of time: years and months and days, and all sorts of time! However, all of those are just named concepts that appear to rational mind. The appearances are just a product of the confusion of rational mind. Thus, they are called "confused appearances".

The things of your world are the appearances of fundamental confusion concerning reality. These appearances of confusion seem to be truly existent but the above shows that they are, in fact, not. They seem to be definitely there but in fact they are not. This absence of the things that appear to be there is called being "empty" of the true existence seen in the confused appearance. The absence in fact of the true existence in the phenomena is called the emptiness of the phenomena.

"Emptiness" does not mean a blank, an absence of all existence. It specifically means absence of true existence. It also does not mean "just empty and nothing else". It also does not mean that one part is removed—made empty—while another part remains established as existent. Emptiness is specifically defined as the type of existence where all things are not truly existent.

You can dream, can't you? You can dream really well. For example, if there is something that you really like, you can dream a dream in which you get that thing effortlessly and with no cost involved. If that happens, you have a really enjoyable time in the dream. However, what if, all of a sudden, a robber appears, beats you, and takes away the thing you like so much? You will dream of the pain of the beating and, being so sad at the loss of the thing you adored so much, you will cry and sob and wail in the dream. When you wake up in the morning, it is even possible that your pillow will be wet from the tears that you shed while dreaming!

So there is the question: what is the principal cause of the joy and the pain and suffering in that kind of dream? It is the article that you were so attached to, isn't it? However, it is not a real thing: it was not made in a factory; didn't have an engineer to design it; was not composed of atoms; and so on. It was just an un-real dream thing. Nonetheless, it was able to produce all of the effects in your mind in the dream, wasn't it? In the dream it was able to be a cause of happiness and a cause of suffering, wasn't it? So the two aspects of not being what it seemed and at the same time appearing there were unified together, weren't they? That is just how it is with all of the phenomena that appear to us now. For example, a cup of tea is not truly existent, and I, the person drinking the tea, am also not truly existent, and the act of drinking the tea is also not truly existent. Nonetheless and like with the things of a dream, if I drink that tea, I can taste it and it can be tasty, too.

In this way, when you analyse the phenomena that appear to you using prajna that gets at the actual situation, you find that they are not truly existent. Moreover, while they are being non-existent in a not truly existent way, they are also apparent, and, while they are being apparent, they are, at the same time, not truly existent. That kind of unified appearance-emptiness is the real meaning of the word "emptiness".

4. The Effect of Meditating on Emptiness

Now, what good will it do to develop experience in emptiness? For example, it is possible to have a very scary dream, one that makes you very afraid. It might be a dream in which a robber robs you or an earthquake makes your house cave in or a car accident. Those kinds of dreams are possible, aren't they? Well, then, what could be done to solve those problems without having to wake up? The best method is to recognize that it is a dream. Other methods such as fighting with the robber, and so on, do not help. Those methods can even make the dream worse; for example, the robber might turn very nasty and harm you badly. Praying to someone in the dream isn't going to help either. In fact, except for actually recognizing that the dream is a dream, these various other methods are not real solutions at all.

If you recognize in a dream that it is a dream, you can then do anything you want in the dream. You could leap off a one-hundred-story building with impunity. You could jump into a fire and not be burned. You could do all of these things because when you realize that the dream is a dream, you realize that all the things of the dream are not truly existent. Since they are not truly existent, how could they inflict any real damage on non-real things, such as your body? All in all, you now have the ability to do many things that you could not have done before. And, you are freed from all fears that you had before, when you were solidifying the dream things into real things. All of this comes from recognizing that the dream is a dream.

The same is true for your present appearances. All of the phenomena that appear to you are not truly existent. They are nothing other than appearances of mind. If you understand that, then you can start the process of purifying all of your confused appearances—which include birth, sickness, old age, and death. As you purify them, you will gradually be released from all of the problems of normal existence—birth, sickness, old age, death, and so on. And not only from the problems of this human life, but you will be gradually released from the problems of every kind of existence that you could take. In other words, the impure appearances of the six types of migrators can be purified out so that they do not happen any longer.

The appearances of the six realms that occur to the six types of migrators who live in them happen solely because those beings do not comprehend the actuality of emptiness. Not comprehending it, all of their impure appearances occur to them. When the actuality of emptiness is comprehended, the appearances turn into appearances of buddha bodies and buddha wisdoms. For example, if the nature of the hells is directly understood to be emptiness, then the container, the hell itself, turns into a buddha field connected with the vajra family and the being within it becomes the buddha of the vajra family, Akshobya.

Thus there is what is called the "equality of samsara and nirvana". Samsara and nirvana appear differently but in fact they have the same entity. We say that samsara is bad and nirvana is good but in reality it is not like that. Why? Because everything of samsara and nirvana is the same in being empty. Because they are both emptiness at root, they are in fact equal. Many people have the idea that a buddha field is up in a high place and is far away but that is incorrect. A buddha field is what you get when you purify your own impure appearances. That is what it is.

The hells and so on are all examples of the impure appearances that occur in sentient beings' impure, dualistic minds. Those places are there simply because sentient beings have created those impure appearances out of their own impurity. In actuality, buddha fields and hell realms both are not truly existent.

Where does this impurity come from? It comes from a bad habit that has been perpetuated from time without beginning in cyclic existence up through the present. That bad habit is the habit of perceiving everything as being truly existent. That habit can be reversed. You have met a guru who tells you that all dharmas are empty. You think about that and, after a while, you start to think that it might be true. Then you become more certain of it. Finally, you are sure that all things really are empty and not truly existent. At that point you have become a buddha.

Some people hear about emptiness and think they will understand it immediately and then, because of that, will be able to jump into a fire and not be burned, and so on. However, it does not work like that. Direct sight of emptiness is needed for that to happen and there is a big difference between direct sight of emptiness and a rational understanding of it. To gain a direct sight of emptiness you have to meditate diligently for a long time. You have to meditate on the antidote to the bad habit perceiving everything as being truly existent, which is emptiness, again and again and again.

5. The Benefits of Meditating on Emptiness

An understanding of emptiness has great meaning. The Buddha said that a person who just once has the suspicion that all phenomena are empty, who just once entertains the thought, "Are they or aren't they empty?" clears out many thousands of aeons of bad deeds. And if that is the case, what need to mention someone who gains certainty that all phenomena are empty? Just by thinking for even one minute that all phenomena are empty, a great accumulation of merit is completed and the bad deeds of hundreds of thousands of aeons are cleared off. The Buddha said that the view of emptiness when well understood is capable of accumulating merit and purifying bad deeds and obscurations.

6. The Actual Meditation on Emptiness

To meditate on emptiness, both shamatha and vipashyana are required. These can be developed independently but finally, in order to directly see emptiness, they must be unified. When the practice is being done, it is called "unifying shamatha and vipashyana".

In general, there are two ways to go about meditating. The first is called analytical meditation and the second is called resting meditation. Analytical meditation is the practice where you sit and think about something, applying your intelligence to it, to try to get to a particular understanding. Resting meditation means that you just settle your mind directly on the understanding that you want to cultivate. Either of these can be applied to meditation on emptiness.

To do analytical meditation on emptiness, you take something like the time and atoms that we talked about before and you investigate it with your mind, trying to come to a direct understanding of the emptiness of phenomena. Some people like this type of meditation and they can do it if they prefer. Other people do not like it so much. For them, they can do resting meditation in which they just rest on the understanding of emptiness that they have developed already. In that case, they think for a little about how all phenomena are empty, how all phenomena are like a dream, how they are like an illusion, then, when they have some feeling of that, they just relax the mind and set it on the meaning that they have found. In the end, a person who does analytical meditation has to do this too. He investigates and investigates, then at the end places his mind on the conclusion that he has come to, and that is resting meditation.

If you practise like that, then, slowly, your meditation will improve, and you will have an increasingly better comprehension of emptiness. At some point you will be certain of emptiness and then it will be possible for you to place your mind right on that certainty and, without being distracted from it, stay there in a relaxed way. If that happens, then that is unified shamatha and vipashyana. The certainty of the meaning is the vipashyana and the staying right on that in a relaxed way without being distracted from it is the shamatha.

You can do the analytical meditation or not, it is up to you, but you must do resting meditation in order to meditate fully on emptiness.

The Main Practice

The Key Point of Mind: Vipashyana

Emptiness Progressively Understood Through the Four Levels of Buddhist Philosophy

The first level of Buddhist philosophy, called the Particularist school, belongs to the Lesser Vehicle. It has a relatively simple presentation of philosophy that is a useful starting point for our development of the intelligence of prajna and the insight of vipashyana. In this system of philosophy, all the phenomena of the fictional level of truth are found in the phenomena that sentient beings believe to be external to mind and in the phenomena they believe to be part of the internal mind. According to the Particularist view, the external phenomena are made up of minute atoms and the internal phenomena of mind are made up of minute moments of consciousness. In other words, in this level of view, subtle atoms and subtle moments of consciousness constitute the whole of phenomena.

These two things, atoms and moments of consciousness form the basis of our confusion. How is that? They are impermanent, made of multiple parts, and dependent on causes, conditions, and other factors but our deluded minds apprehend them as permanent, singular, and independent. For example, there is yourself who you call "I", "me"; you grasp at that with your rational mind[33] and in doing so see yourself as a permanent, singular, and independent thing. You think, "I am really here" and in doing so think that you are permanent. You think, "I'm here myself" and in doing so think of yourself as one, single, individualized thing. When you do this, you also think that you are independent, not dependent on causes, conditions, parts, and other factors that go into your makeup.

These three mis-apprehensions are delusions in their own right. However, they are also symptoms of the fundamental delusion, the ignorance that grasps things as being truly existent. Nonetheless, as explained earlier, we can start by applying prajna at the level of the mis-apprehensions of permanence, and so on. Then, by seeing that they are mistaken, it clears up the surface level of delusion, making it easier to apply prajna to the fundamental ignorance.

Let's start with apprehending permanence in phenomena. An example of this is the thought, "I am the child of this woman who is my mother". Why? Because you are no longer the small child that was born of your mother. When you say, "I", it should apply to something that actually exists doesn't it? The present thing that you think of as being yourself is larger isn't it? The thing that was born from your mother was quite small and does not exist any longer. If you see somebody whom you were introduced to many years ago, you will think, "That is so and so", but that is a mistaken thought because the

---

[33] Tib. blo. Rational mind is a name for mind that emphasizes its dualistic quality.

present object of visual consciousness is not the person you met before. In another example, you have lost your watch and found it again and put it on your wrist; you will think, "This is my watch, the one I lost before", and be thinking that it is one and the same thing but it is not. In another example, you saw a vase two years ago and didn't see it again until today but your thought will be, "Oh today, I saw that vase again that I haven't seen for two years", but the vase has changed and is not the exact same vase that you saw before. This seeing of something as always being the same thing, regardless of the fact that it is in fact impermanent, is the mis-apprehending permanence in things that are impermanent.

Buddha said that all compounded things are impermanent and pointed out that there are two levels of their impermanence. The first, subtle impermanence, is that impermanent things are changing from moment to moment to moment. Modern day scientists say the same. Take the example just mentioned of a watch that you lost. There is nothing about a watch that stays the same from moment to moment. From the instant that a watch has been made in the factory, it is always changing a little and getting older. It never stays exactly the same as before. This is its subtle impermanence. The second, coarse impermanence refers to the obvious level of change, such as a watch breaking, or stopping, or seasons changing. This level always occurs on the basis of the subtle level of impermanence.

When you apprehend things as permanent, that is part of the fictional level of reality but it is not correct even at the fictional level. Therefore it is called wrong or upside-down fiction and is not true at all. If you see those same things but apprehend them as subtly impermanent, then those things are part of the fictional level of reality and are true at that level.

Therefore it is called fictional truth. In other words, your overall context is obscuration producing a fiction but within that you can apprehend a thing in a way which is or is not correct. The apprehension of impermanent things is correct at the fictional level.

Then, what is the apprehension of things as singular? Think about the "I" again. You see yourself as one, single thing. When you think "I" or "me", you only think of yourself as a singular thing, not as multiple things, don't you? Likewise with a watch. When you think of a watch, you think of it as one, singular thing, not as a multiplicity of things put together. Or, say that there are ten pens laid out together. You don't think of those pens as ten, individual things but see them as being one thing, "the ten pens". This is called, "apprehending things as singular". Of the two truths, that is just fiction. It is not true, even at its own level so is also called "wrong fictional truth" or, literally, "topsy-turvy fictional truth".

What does it mean that things are not singular? For example, "I" myself am multiple things; I am not one, singular thing the way I think I am. Scientists will agree that a table, for instance, is not really the solid, single thing that we apprehend in our perception of the table but is a collection of atoms all moving around. They will point out that the "solid" table is not solid but is just waves moving and interacting. We make a mistake about the table and also make the same mistake about ourselves. Thus, there is no singular thing anywhere at all, including for our sense "I".

Why are things not there as singular entities? Because they have parts to them. If something is made of parts, it cannot be a singular thing, can it? This is a very important point of reasoning. Look at yourself. You are made up of lots of parts, aren't you? You have two arms, two legs, a head. You have a skeleton with three hundred and sixty odd bones in it. You have many different organs. You have flesh, skin, muscles, and so on. At the more subtle level, you have 21,000 channels and 21,000 kinds of winds travelling in them. And that is still a coarse way of looking at it because, if you consider the hairs and hair pores, there are millions of them. Thus, you are not a singular thing but a multiplicity of many different things put together.

Then, you will also find that you apprehend the things of your world as independent. If you look at a watch, you will find that you take it to be something that exists in its own right, without any further relationship to its parts, causes, or the world surrounding it. Likewise, if you can get a sense of the "I" that you think you have, you will find that you take it to be independent, existing in its own right. However, all things arise as interdependent things, being produced through a complex interdependency of causes, conditions, parts, and other factors. Thus, if you examine things carefully, you will find that they are dependent things, arising in dependence on various causes and inter-relationships. Again, the apprehension of independence is mere fiction, topsy-turvy fictional truth.

The reason for this discussion is that, if you want to arrive at the superfactual truth, you first have to get past the mere fiction that you impose on fictional truth and get at least to the fictional truth itself. That is the first step towards fully understanding reality. I have said that all of the phenomena there are, comprised of atomic particles and moments of consciousness, are at the level of fictional truth. You apprehend these things made up from these atomic particles and moments of consciousness as permanent, singular, and independent. However, when you examine carefully, as we have been doing, you find that they are not that way. It is not their actual situation.

Thus you, as a person, are a compounded phenomenon. You are not permanent, singular, and dependent but impermanent, multiple, and independent. The first three apprehensions are fictions which are just wrong and the second three are the same thing but seen properly, that is, they are the fictional truth.

Till now, we have been discussing the Lesser Vehicle approach to reality in which the correction of the mis-apprehension of fictional truth is a step towards understanding emptiness of a personal self. In the Lesser Vehicle, you can also apply those teachings to finding the emptiness of a personal self and if you succeed in that, you liberate yourself from cyclic existence by reaching the stage of an arhat. However, that is not the end of the journey; you still have to go all the way to the enlightenment of a truly complete buddha and for that there are the sutra teachings of the Great Vehicle, and especially of the Prajnaparamita, which emphasize that all phenomena, both a personal self and all other phenomena, are empty. Beyond that, there are the teachings of the Vajra Vehicle. These do not show a deeper level of emptiness than the sutra Great Vehicle; the Great Vehicle Prajnaparamita teachings fully show the emptiness of all phenomena. However, they are more direct in the way that they show the ultimate level of truth in which appearance and emptiness, or the two truths, are unified.

Thus, Buddhist philosophy contains many levels of understanding of reality. The reason for this is because, as the Buddha said, different beings have different constitutions and differing levels of intelligence and to accommodate those differing levels he gave different levels of presentation of reality. There are four main schools of Buddhist philosophy at the sutra level; there are two in the Lesser Vehicle and two in the Great Vehicle. The coarsest presentation of reality is found in the Lesser Vehicle school called the Particularists. A subtler approach but still in the Lesser Vehicle school is called the Sautrantika, "The Followers of Sutra". The next more subtle presentation is found in the Cittamatra, "Mind Only" school, of the Great Vehicle and the most subtle presentation is found in the Madhyamaka, "The Middle Way" school of the Great Vehicle. Beyond these ways of explaining the teachings in the sutra system, there is, for people with even sharper abilities, the presentations of the esoteric or tantra schools, all of which belong to the Vajra Vehicle.

The Particularists proclaim that external subtle atoms and internal moments of consciousness are ultimate truths. They also proclaim that all of these are subtly impermanent. However, they assert this impermanence very strongly and in doing so turn it into a kind of permanence. They arrive at an emptiness just of the personal self. The next level up, the Sutra Followers, do not push the issue of momentariness so strongly and their presentation is more subtle. By it, they arrive not only at an emptiness of the personal self but a partial understanding of the emptiness of other phenomena as well. The next step up, the Mind Only followers, look carefully into both the personal self and the rest of phenomena and so do come to a determination of emptiness both of self and phenomena. However, they have some fixation on the nature of the mind that knows emptiness so it is said that their understanding of two-fold emptiness is still flawed.

How do the Mind Only followers arrive at the determination that atoms are empty? Generally the lower two schools are able to determine that atoms and likewise moments of consciousness are momentarily existent. It is said that they can arrive at "impermanent partlessness" and there is a major point of understanding here. They maintain that there is a kind of subtle atom which is momentarily impermanent but has no parts to it. How do they get to that determination? They approach it by seeing that things can only exist in the present moment and they refine that present moment down to the most minute instant of time that there could be. If they went further, they would find that the momentary, partless atoms are empty but they do not continue because of fear. They are afraid that everything would disappear and that there would be no cause and effect. They edge into the emptiness but stop short because of their fear. So the two, lower schools stop at partless atoms as their ultimate truths. However, the Mind Only followers keep going where the lower two schools stopped. They analyse the situation more deeply and point out that the lower schools were being too coarse in their analysis. They point out that anything that there is, including the most subtle atom, has sides to it and because it has sides to it, it does have parts. In that way, the Mind Only followers arrive at a much deeper understanding of emptiness. They get to full emptiness for external atoms because they allow them to have parts; if anything has parts then it will, by logical analysis, definitely turn out to be empty of a fixed entity. However, they do not get to a full emptiness for the mind that sees reality because they proclaim a kind of ultimate existence for that particular type of knower.

Now what does it mean to be fully empty, that is, empty in the way that the Great Vehicle claims things to be empty? If something has parts to it, in other words if it is not partless, then it can be dissected into its pieces. That in turn means that the thing made up of parts is not really there and that not-really-there-ness is the emptiness of the thing. Empty means "devoid of" and when talking about either a personal self or a self in phenomena it means that the phenomenon is not really there the way we see it, which is that we see it with a self. Emptiness means that phenomena are not there the way they seem.[34]

For example, if you look into your mind and try to find how you apprehend your "I", you will see that it appears as a singular thing, a solid lump without parts. In fact, this "I" cannot be one thing the way that it appears to us; it has to be many things. There are many reasons why this is so, but one of them is that the "I" is connected with the five skandhas or aggregates. It has to be connected with the five aggregates because our whole psycho-physical being is none other than the five aggregates and the "I" is supposedly a reference to our psycho-physical being[35]. However, when you look through

---

[34] The Indian Buddhist tradition developed five, main types of logic for determining that there is not a personal self nor a self in other phenomena in the way that we ordinary beings see that there is one. The logic involved in the discussions about partless atoms and the other reasonings given below come from just those five, main types of logic. These reasonings all lead to the notion that the personal self, an "I" does not, in fact, exist and that the same kind of self in other things also does not exist.

[35] A complete presentation of the five aggregates is given in the book published by PKTC called *The Six Topics That All Buddhists*
(continued...)

the five aggregates, you cannot find this kind of "I" anywhere within them. At that point, you have realized the emptiness of a personal self. Another way of doing it is to say that the "I" is connected with your total makeup, which consists of body, speech, and mind. However, it couldn't be in the body because, if you look, you will find that the singular thing "I" that you discovered when you looked for it is not in the arms, not in the legs, and not in any part of the body anywhere. It couldn't be in the speech because the speech is just a constantly changing series of sound patterns that sometimes is not even operating and that kind of singular "I" cannot be found in there, either. Then, it is not in the mind because mind is just a constant stream of events and the "I" was a singular, permanent thing. It is also not the sum of the five aggregates or the sum of body, speech, and mind. Each of the parts of the body is not the "I", is it? If the individual parts are not the "I", then to say that the whole thing is the "I" is a mistake. Despite this lack of findability, the "I" does appear very strongly to your mind. What does that mean? It means that the "I" is just something that your mind has grasped onto. It is an exaggeration over what is really there. It does not exist as it appears. It is empty.

Take a hand. You would say that it is a hand, but actually it is just a collection of parts. Each part is not the hand, is it? Then, going more finely, take the thumb. Cut the thumb into parts. Each of those is not the thumb is it? Then take each of those and cut it into a further eight pieces. Is any one of them the thumb? Then keep going like that and eventually you will get down to the atoms comprising the hand. Each of those atoms has sides and parts to it, doesn't it? Therefore each of

---

[35](...continued)
Learn, 2012, 978-9937-572-13-2.

those can be broken down further. Even if you were to reduce the atoms down to waves, which some physicists would do, a wave still has a top and a bottom. Is the top part of the wave, the wave? No. Is the bottom part of the wave, the wave? No. So there is no wave there, either. You can go even further. There is matter and anti-matter and if the two meet, they cancel each other out and disappear, but if atoms are truly permanent—which is one of the qualities of a fixed self—then meeting cannot happen. So, in the end, when you get down to it, there are no truly existent atoms, are there?

If you think about it, the only reason that we say we have hair is because there are individual hairs to start with. If the individual hairs were not present, you could not have a head of hair. It is the same with a forest: a forest is there only because there are trees; if there were no trees, then there would be no forest. Given that that is how compounded things are, and since we agreed that everything is made up of atoms, and since there are no atoms, this all means that there is not anything here. Everything is just a play of confusion.

So far we have been investigating external atoms. An investigation of moments of consciousness brings a similar result. The moments of consciousness are, from the standpoint of fictional truth, impermanent, and those impermanent moments of consciousness are, from the standpoint of superfactual truth, empty. How do we determine that these moments of consciousness are empty? We can do it using time. Consciousness the way we normally think about it really is an obscured way of thinking about it. We think that it is there and that it goes along from moment to moment. However, if you examine it more carefully: past consciousness does not exist—it is gone; future consciousness has not yet happened so it does not exist either; and if there were such a thing as partless moment of consciousness, it would have to exist in the present moment. However, when you analyse to find a present moment, you cannot find that, either. Therefore mind also is empty.

Generally speaking, we think we have consciousness. If there is consciousness, it has to be something that exists at the fictional level of truth. At that level, you would consider that consciousness was something that existed from moment to moment. However, it could be examined to see whether it exists superfactually or not. To do that, you can examine it using parts theory with time, as mentioned above. If there were such a thing as a consciousness that existed in time, it would have to be existent in the present moment because, as we have seen above, past consciousness and future consciousness do not exist. The Particularists say that the present moment of consciousness is an ultimate truth; it is a superfactual truth for them because they say the present moment of consciousness is partless and cannot be divided further. This is as far as they go. It is a coarse realization of emptiness. The Mind Only followers agree that external atoms are empty because they accept that external atoms have parts, however they do not accept that the mind of realization has parts and they are stuck there.

This brings us then to the fourth of the schools of Buddhist philosophy, the Madhyamaka or Middle Way. The followers of the Middle Way say that not only external atoms but also moments of consciousness must have parts. They give the reason that any present moment of consciousness has a past and future moment of consciousness impinging on it, thus a present moment of consciousness has the parts of past and future moments. If there is a present moment of consciousness, there has to be a connection between the present moment and the future or past moments. If there is, then the present moment has to include the past and future moments of consciousness—the related past and future moments would all have to be included in the present moment. However, the present moment does not include them. If you continue with the analysis, you cannot find a present moment of consciousness that exists as a thing. Therefore the consciousness also becomes non-existent. Thus, for the Middle Way followers, there is no consciousness either.

You might then say that the Middle Way followers have fallen into the extreme of nihilism because they have eliminated everything—both external atoms and internal consciousnesses. However, that is not the case. It does not happen because the Middle Way followers say that, even though these things do not really exist, they still appear in a confused way, like an illusion, like a dream. It is like a house in a dream. Is a house in a dream really there? You see the house fully and clearly, and it does function as a house in the dream but is there one normal atom of a house there at all? You might dream that you have accumulated every dollar in the world but when you wake up, how many dollars do you have? In a dream, even though you do not have a house or are not getting the dollars, you still dream that you do have the house or do have the dollars and, in the same way, it is explained that all of the things that appear to us are like in a dream. Thus, at this final level, all phenomena both external and internal are found at the superfactual level to be not-existent but they do appear and operate at the fictional level, like a dream. Thus, at the most subtle presentation of reality in Buddhism, there is no falling into the extreme of permanence because all things are seen to be empty and equally there is no falling into the other extreme of nihilism because phenomena still do appear and do operate as interdependent arisings. Because it falls into neither extreme, this presentation is known as "The Middle Way".

The Main Practice

The Key Point of Mind: Vipashyana

Emptiness Known Through An Examination of Time

If you do not look closely at things, if you just take whatever suddenly appears to you without any further analysis, you would have to say, "Well, things do exist!" That raises the question, "Where do they exist?" If we look at this using time, then, since there is no past and no future, they could only exist in the present moment.

Why is there no past? Because the past has stopped. For example, if you burn paper in a fire, then its gone, isn't it? If a person dies, then he is not there any longer is he? The point here is that when something is finished, it has ceased and is no longer present. If something has ceased, can it be present? Think about it and see if there is anything that you can think of that persists even after it has finished and ceased.

Why is there no future? Because the future has not yet happened. A child that is not born yet cannot be said to exist. A watch not yet manufactured, cannot be said to exist. If a house has not been built yet, then you cannot say that the house exists. Because of this reasoning, you could not possibly say that a future thing exists.

Therefore, we conclude that whatever exists, exists only in the present moment. However if you examine even the present moment carefully, you find that it also is made up of earlier and later moments. In the end, if you keep examining the present moment, you find that there is no present moment that exists either. And, if you examine the momentary things that seem to exist in the present moment, you discover that they too cannot be found to exist in the way that they appear. Thus, there is no past, present, or future and so things that are seen to exist in any of the three also do not exist. The absence of time and things when scrutinized by methods such as this is their emptiness. That time and things do appear is the fictional level of truth. That they are empty is the superfactual truth. That they in fact are empty as they appear and appear while being empty is their ultimate truth. In this way, the ultimate truth of phenomena is the union of the two truths.[36]

---

[36] That is how Buddha explained the entirety of existence with the teaching of the two truths. He said that there is no other possibility; everything is either a fictional truth or a superfactual truth. Fictional truths are the various realities made up by beings with obscured minds. All the phenomena experienced by obscured mind are fictional truths; all of them are phenomena made up by the obscuration in the dualistic mind of sentient beings. Fictional here is a word that means "a product only of obscuration". All of these phenomena are empty and that is their superfactual truth. In the sutras, superfactual truth is stated to be the emptiness of phenomena which is seen in the equipoise of noble beings. In other words, it is a *superior* truth that is *factual*

(continued...)

The Main Practice

The Key Points of Mind:

Vajra Vehicle Meditations on Reality

I have discussed shamatha meditation and meditation on emptiness according to the way that they are done conventionally. This conventional approach is taught in the sutras of the Buddha. There is a higher kind of meditation, as I mentioned at the beginning of the instruction on shamatha. This is the kind of meditation taught in Mahamudra and Great Completion traditions. It is the practice of the essence of mind. This is not usually something that beginners can do well. Most people need to develop shamatha and then meditation on emptiness, as described above. When that is in place, the final type of meditation, meditation on the essence of mind, can also go well. Because of this, meditation on the essence of mind is not usually presented to beginners, and accordingly,

---

[36](...continued)
for noble, meaning spiritually advanced, beings. Superfactual truth is not the product of obscuration; it is factual and it is superior, more so than the fictional truth that sentient beings create with their obscured minds.

it is not discussed here. Nonetheless, in this chapter, there is a technique of shamatha practice that follows the style of these higher meditations, which will be presented here. After that, a brief introduction to the style of the higher meditations, emphasizing the relaxation aspect, will be given.

1. Threefold Abiding, Moving, and Knowing

There is a practice in the Mahamudra system called "Threefold abiding, moving, and knowing". If you practise it, it can result in you introducing yourself to the nature of your own mind, which is vipashyana. In other words it is possible for this style of shamatha practice to turn into the real, unified shamatha-vipashyana practice of Mahamudra and Great Completion. It is a method in which the ground of mind or enlightened core could be apprehended based just on doing shamatha practice; if the practice goes well then it is possible to have a direct comprehension of the essence of mind by starting out with shamatha practice.

The name of the practice comes because three things of abiding, moving, and knowing are present in your mind when doing meditation: at times mind abides, meaning that it simply abides without producing thoughts; at times it moves, meaning that it is not abiding calmly but is producing thoughts; and in either case it has the general quality of knowing and that knowing can be used to know whether it is abiding or moving. Overall, our minds are doing one of two things: they are either moving or not moving—which is called abiding. There is never a situation where it is not moving and not abiding; such a possibility does not exist.

It is easy to take abiding and turn it into meditation. Many people think, "Oh, now my mind is calm, not moving, this is really excellent meditation". These people usually do not want thoughts and darkness coming into their peaceful meditation because they see these as enemies of their meditation. They end up rejecting these things as part of meditation and because of that are not able to turn discursive thought and so on into meditation. And, for anyone who is not able to take discursive thoughts and so on and turn them into meditation, meditation will always be difficult. It will be difficult for this kind of person really to become a meditator.

Thus, we need a method that will allow discursive thought—feelings, afflictions and so on, everything that comes into mind because of its contact with the objects of the senses—to be turned into meditation. Six meditations were mentioned earlier and five of them explained. Now, for the sixth, which is the method that will allow the whole net of discursive thought to be turned into meditation. The other meditations were shamatha practice done in regard to each of the five sense objects. This meditation is shamatha meditation done in regard to mental sense objects, which is discursive thought in its variety. This meditation is easy. When the eye is seeing visual form, together with that, if the mind also observes the form, then that becomes a support of non-distraction for the mind. Likewise, if the mind listens to sounds, then the sound becomes a support for mind's non-distraction. As your senses know visual form, sound and so on, your mind will tend to produce thoughts about those things and will become distracted. That means, that, to do the practice, you have to come closer to discursive thought.

Thinking that the essence of discursive thought is emptiness will not help. Thinking anything about the discursive thought will not help. No further thinking is required when dealing with discursive thought. Rather, if you know the discursive thought as it comes, then just by that you will not be distracted from the discursive thought and that is the practice. No matter what discursiveness comes into mind, stay right with that. Do not be distracted from it. It is not that you have to focus on a specific thought. In any given moment, if there is discursive thought, there is just one thing, and you allow yourself to be aware of that. One discursive thought will come and then usually a second and third following it. Discursive thoughts are like the beads on a necklace; they come one at a time, one after another. So, if you are just aware of a thought when it comes, then that thought itself becomes a support for the non-distracted-ness of mind. That is how you do it.

The abiding part that was mentioned first is easy, it is not the whole story. Some people think that is the whole meditation. They tend to be averse to things that disturb their meditation. If you are meditating and something comes up and you find yourself being averse to it because it is disturbing your meditation, take just that thought of aversion as the point of practice. It could be a simple thought or anything that comes—feelings, afflictions—on the basis of contact with any of the six senses. If you can just be aware of it and not allow it to be a cause of further distraction then that thing, whether it is a simple thought, a feeling, an affliction or whatever, will turn into shamatha practice itself. If you are angry, so angry that you want to beat someone, then take the anger as the basis for the practice.

There are two parts to this. The first is that you have to recognize that a thought has arisen in the moment that it arises. The second, which is equally important but the main work, is that you have to look at the thought. Look at here does not mean look into its essence, it just means to be with the thought as it comes, stays, and goes. Then, if you do that, any thought, including deep anger, becomes the way to remain undistracted. When you practise non-distraction, that eventually leads to one-pointedness of mind, which is the point of shamatha practice.

One of the qualities of shamatha practice is that there is a split into observer and observed. When some people hear this, they think it is a fault because they have not studied shamatha practice by itself; they have only heard about the higher practices where there is not supposed to be a duality of observer and observed. However, shamatha practice alone is not a non-dual practice and it is a necessary part of that practice that there is both an observer and observed in it.

In shamatha, the observer is more like an examiner; something that is looking at and knowing the content of mind in any given moment. This examiner is a quality of knowing that is present in the mind. This could be called mindfulness though, in the phrase we are talking about, it is the third one of the three, and is called "knowing". It looks at and sees anything that arises in mind, discursive thought and everything that it entails, feeling and affliction, and so on.

As the knower does its job of looking and seeing, it might discriminate that one kind of thought is good and another is bad and another is in-between. However, it does not do anything with this discrimination. In other words, it knows the content of mind from moment to moment but does not then call out to the mind and say, "Hey! This thought is good, you should keep it or follow it", and likewise it does not call out to the mind and say, "Hey! This thought is bad, you should not keep it or follow it". For example, when you have "bad" thoughts such as a desire to harm someone else, the knower will see that. The important thing at that time is not to turn outwards towards the object of the angry thought. If you did that, it would produce a whole train of fantasy, for example about someone you want to harm. Rather, it is important for the mind to stay turned inwards and to keep looking at the thought itself, in this case an angry thought that wants to harm others. The same is true for "good" thoughts. Just because they are good, you might think that it is all right to be led away by them. However, the practice is to stay with the content of mind, whatever it is, good, bad, or in-between.

Thus, for this practice whatever arises in the mind is all right. Angry thoughts are all right, lusty thoughts are all right, and so on. Because of this, you can go wherever you go and be at ease. Anywhere you go, you can stay with the impressions of the senses as described in the first five meditations which brings the peaceful state of shamatha, even in a busy town. And then, if you use this sixth practice in conjunction with it, no matter what thoughts, feelings, or even afflictions arise because of your sensory experiences, you will be able to stay right with them. Not only will they not turn into samsaric problems for you, but they will be turned into the opposite—they will become the cause of peaceful mind that is helpful right in the present and which will help you when you do the practice of unified shamatha-vipashyana that looks into reality and ultimately frees you from cyclic existence.

In the practice of "threefold abiding, moving, and knowing", if you do the practice as described above and look again and again at mind to see is it abiding, is it moving, then it is possible that the knower, which in this case is a coarse, separate observer, might dissolve and the knower which is innate to the essence of mind might come forth. If that happens, the essence of whatever abiding happens is the knower and the essence of whatever moving happens is the knower. Thus, the abiding and the movement come to have the same essence, which is mind's innate knower. The abiding and movement are said to be not different at that point in the sense that they are both manifestations of the innate knower of mind.

When that happens, conventional meditation disappears. A person who was doing shamatha practice and has this happen to them will feel that he has lost the meditation. The beginner will think that they have lost their meditation or that it has gone wrong. Actually, they have lost the meditation but this is not bad. It is called "no-meditation" and corresponds to the fact that, at the higher levels of practice, there is no conventional meditation to be done. The sort of meditation that happens is one in which there is no separate observer and observed. When this happens, the practitioner returns to a very basic state of mind[37]. Because of that, the kind of mind that opens up here is called "common mind"[38]. So, if this really does happen, it is the best kind of meditation. At that point, the essence of mind really has come forth into direct experience for the practitioner. The insight into reality which is naturally occurring at that time is called vipashyana and the

---

[37] Basic here means the state of mind that is common to all sentient beings, before all of the extra stuff of dualistic mind happened.

[38] Tib. tha mal gyi shes pa. Sometimes this is translated as "ordinary mind" but that is not the meaning of the term. It means the awareness that is common to everyone, before all the baggage of dualistic mind appeared.

abiding in it that is naturally occurring is called shamatha, though this is the nature of mind itself which is an un-constructed state that is true shamatha and vipashyana that cannot be separated from each other.

2. A Small Introduction To Mahamudra and Great Completion Meditation

The meditation practice of the higher tantras that is, of Mahamudra and Great Completion, is not the kind where you create something with your mind for example, it is not like using mind to develop loving kindness. Rather, it is a style of meditation in which nothing is created but in which what you have already, your own nature, is allowed to come out. This is called non-meditation style of meditation.

The non-meditation style of practice does involve shamatha but it always uses shamatha without reference. In it, there is no reference made to some other object in order to make the mind abide, rather, the meditating mind itself is used as the basis for the shamatha.

For the non-meditation style of practice, one of the greatest key points of mind is for the mind to be relaxed. Because of this, the word "shamatha" meaning calm abiding is used when the higher tantras speak of meditation but they have many other special words for the relaxation of mind which they tend to use instead.

Having shamatha or relaxation is a key point, an exceptionally important part, of the non-meditation style of practice. Therefore, here is a sense of how this kind of relaxation should be, given through the example of a running race. These days, long-distance foot races are popular in the United States. Many people come together, run a long distance, and whoever comes first gets a large cash prize. Imagine that you have entered one of these races. The night before you will be keyed up thinking about the possibility of winning the cash prize the next day. The morning of the race, you will be out at the start line with the others, thinking "I need to win". The starting gun goes off and you are racing! You run and run and get really sweaty and tired but, in the end, you do win. You are really pleased at winning and especially at getting the prize but are really exhausted so you go home. At home you have a hot bath and then sink into a comfortable chair, heave a deep sigh, and just totally let go and relax, nothing bothering you at all because you are pleased at having won the race. This kind of total relaxation and ease of mind is the sort of relaxation I am talking about in this kind of meditation.

The way to do this kind of meditation is very much like just sitting there using only the key points of the body described in the last chapter. You arrange your body using the key points but don't think about them any further and just relax in that state, as in the example above. You are not meditating, meaning you are not using your mind to create something in the normal way of meditation. At the same time, your mind is totally at ease and utterly present. There is no meditation to be done; all that is to be done is to rest, allowing whatever comes into mind to come, but without wandering from the present. Altogether, this kind of meditation does not require any special practice. Unlike normal meditation where you have to use your intellect to create something, there is also no need for thinking about anything. The state that you sit within is a dimensionless, naked experience, so there is no need to be thinking about how it should be. If you think a lot about how the state should be—for instance, because of having been told that it is dimensionless, you sit there thinking to yourself that there is no centre, no edge, and so on—then you lose the state itself. In this kind of non-meditation meditation, the constant inspection of mind that is needed in ordinary types of meditation is totally un-necessary.

If you sum up this kind of non-meditation style of meditation, there are two key points that describe it: "no distraction" and "no meditation". These key points convey the meaning that, if you can sit there with none of the normal kind of concept-filled meditation, yet can sit there totally undistracted from the immediacy of the present moment, then, even though there is no "meditation" happening, that is all that is needed.

"No distraction" means that you have to rest naturally, that you leave things be as they are. Beginners often feel that they will "lose track" or "lose themselves" if they do this. However, you will not lose yourself, rather, you will be more fully present than normal! Actually, "distraction" is when you lose yourself; you become lost in thought during your meditation and someone else says something to you and you say "What?!" as you come back from your non-existent fantasy world and regain your bearings in the present. In this kind of "no distraction" meditation there is none of that; there is just a constant remaining in the present. You do lose one thing; you do lose beating your head against the wall, thinking about this and that, which is the style of normal meditation in which you are using your mind to create something.

"No meditation" means that our minds are naturally illuminative of themselves, like a lamp, so nothing more is needed than allowing the natural luminosity of the mind to shine forth. A lamp, just by being present, illuminates itself because of its own luminosity. No matter how much darkness there is, the lamp will illuminate itself—you do not need to turn on another light to find it—and mind is just the same. In fact, the name given to this basic illuminative quality of mind, the basic quality of knowing is exactly "luminosity"[39].

This level of the knowing quality of mind does not have to have an object of knowledge, such as an object of the senses, for its operation. This level of knowing is our innermost nature which has the quality of just knowing. Since this is our nature, it does not need to be brought about through meditation where meditation means producing a new state of mind and then cultivating it. Thus it is brought forth by non-meditation, the process of just allowing it to be present.

This knower is our nature; we do have it. If we did not have it, then we would have to produce it by a process of creative meditation such as the meditation on a deity. For example, in the meditation of Vajrasatva, you have to create all of the different parts by deliberately thinking about them. When beginners do this, they picture one part such as the head, then lose another part such as the feet, then they re-picture the feet but lose the hands, and so on. It is a very manual process of creation. However in "no meditation" meditation practice, we are not trying to create something using the process of medita-

---

[39] See the glossary. This has been mistakenly called "clear light" for many years now. Unfortunately, "clear light" is very misleading; it gives many people the idea that there is some kind of light in the mind. In fact, the Sanskrit word is a metaphor for the simple fact of knowing. It is the same as the English word "illumination" used for the same purpose for example, "he had a moment of illumination".

tion. There is no need to do that because we have, as our very nature, the knower that we want to bring into manifestation.

In the non-meditation practice that stays undistracted from the luminosity nature of mind, all that is needed is to recognize the luminosity to begin with then rest within that knower that has been recognized.

It is that simple. There is nothing whatsoever to do. There is nothing to think about at all. There is nothing to be created. There is nothing at all needed. Nevertheless, through this nothing to be done at all approach, every possible good quality can and does come. It is easier than drinking water from a glass; in this there is nothing to do, but in drinking water from a glass you have to raise it to your lips, drink from the glass, then swallow and finally put the glass back down. Nothing is needed for it, but for beginners the experience of it will not stay for very long.

If you continue to rest relaxed in this nature of mind, your experience of it will become steadier and, at that point, your meditation will have become good and you will be able to stay in it for a long period. Without that kind of training, it is not possible to stay in it for more than one or two seconds. However, that is not a bad state of affairs, in fact, it is the reason why there is this instruction for beginners that meditation should be done in "short periods, many times". Since beginners cannot stay in the state for long periods, any attempt to meditate in it for long periods will result in the meditation not going well at best and usually the meditation will fall either into sinking and dullness or agitation of one kind or another. Therefore beginners should not think, "I will meditate for long periods", but should think, "I will meditate for short periods"; if you think to yourself, "Being in this kind of state for just a second is enough", then your meditation will come along well. If you think, "I *will* meditate for a long time", and really push and try, the meditation will not turn out well.

Nevertheless, a slight sense of determination about your meditation is useful. What is the value of doing this using "short periods"? It is that the faults of sinking and agitation will not come. What is the value of doing this using "many times"? It is that the meditation will improve. Thereby both of the needs for meditation are fulfilled. Other than that, having the idea that you should do it for long periods and that you should really exert yourself to make it happen in one session will not be productive.

The last paragraph explains the practice of Mahamudra called Essence Mahamudra and of Great Completion called The Thorough Cut[40]. It is important to understand that there is a difference between non-referencing shamatha meditation *per se* and the Mahamudra and Great Completion practices. The difference is that there is what is called "recognizing" in the latter two whereas there is no "recognizing" in the first. In Essence Mahamudra and The Thorough Cut, you recognize the essence of your own mind then rest in that without altering it.

In non-referencing shamatha, you do not recognize then rest in the essence of your own mind but simply rest in your mind without distraction from it. This is a big difference! The difference is like this: if you stand in front of a full-length mirror, your whole body will appear in it as a reflection, and,

---

[40] See the glossary.

if someone just glances at that, they will see a reflection that really does appear to them to be you and it would be possible for them to mistake that mere reflection for the actual, solid person with blood, flesh, bones, brain, heart, and all of the other parts of a physical body. The difference between that mere reflection which seems to be it and the actual thing is like night and day, and the difference between shamatha without signs and Essence Mahamudra and Thorough Cut is just as large.

Now some people think that the practice described in the instruction,

> Not following after the past,
> Not going forth to greet the future,
> But resting self-settled in the present.

is the practice of Thorough Cut when in fact it is a particular set of instructions on the practice of shamatha without reference. Unfortunately many people in the West these days make this mistake. There are Westerners who study with Hindu masters and then Buddhist masters and claim that they are practising Great Completion when in fact they have not understood this key difference. And amongst Buddhists, there are many Westerners who follow the Hinayana Schools, such as the followers in the "Vipassana" groups, and then study Great Completion but who do not understand this key difference. There are followers of Great Completion who make this mistake, too. The purpose of Essence Mahamudra and Thorough Cut is to bring forth the luminosity of mind, yet the kind of practice just mentioned would not bring it forth. All in all, there is a great need to understand properly just what shamatha practice is and how it sits in relation to the practices of all of the vehicles of Buddhism. In particular, if you want to bring forth luminosity, there is a great need to understand the particular styles of shamatha that are used within Essence Mahamudra and again within The Thorough Cut and to learn where they are the same and where they differ from other styles of shamatha.

This of course does not mean that you should be thinking about these things while actually doing the practice; while doing the practice you should not be thinking over the practice but just resting relaxed. Then, if the practice becomes shamatha, so be it. If it becomes the Mahamudra yoga of one-pointedness, so be it. If it becomes the resting aspect of The Thorough Cut, so be it. If it becomes unified shamatha-vipashyana of Essence Mahamudra or The Thorough Cut, so be it. The approach of Essence Mahamudra and Thorough Cut is to abandon all conceptual approaches to the meditation, so that it really does become non-meditation.

Thus, for these highest levels of practice, you take the approach that, wherever it takes you, so be it. If it takes you to hell, so you go to hell. If the practice is mistaken, so be it, it is mistaken. If it is not mistaken, so be it, it is not mistaken. Wherever it takes you, it takes you. That approach is crucial. And since it is that way, it is easy; there is nothing difficult about it at all. Look, if you take your finger and try to touch space with it, what happens?! You poke your finger here and there but every time you move it, it has already touched space before you even move it! Why? Because it is already within space! It is already in contact with space!

Therefore, this practice is exceptionally easy. Well, there is one difficulty! It is so easy that it is difficult. It is so easy that it is hard to trust in the reality of it. We tend to think, "It must be something else" other than what is right before us. We conceptually think in the middle of the meditation, "Very spacious. Very vast. This present mind is nothing at all", and in doing so lose trust in what is right before us. It is very close to us but it is so close that we just cannot see it.

Now, if you do meditate using those instructions, meditation can be done anywhere, anytime. For example, you can meditate while watching television. Thus, the usual approach of "Oh, I am free to meditate now", and "Oh, I'm too busy, I cannot meditate just now", is not applicable here. You can do this practice anytime, for example when you are drinking tea, when the advertisements come along while watching television, and so on. The reason for this is that your nature, your innate disposition is one of relaxation. Because that is your nature, you can let it come forth at any time, in any circumstance.

The Conclusion

Dedication, the Seal

The tradition speaks of three types of dedication:

> Best: dedication done without referencing the sphere of three;
> Middling: dedication done that follows the way shown by others;
> Least: dedication done with poison attached.

The first is the best. However, until you are able to stay within the essence of mind while doing it, until you can stay in the direct perception of emptiness of the three parts involved in the dedication, of dedicator, act of dedication, and the thing dedicated to, then it is not possible to do a dedication at this level. This corresponds to the dedication of a very advanced practitioner. Generally speaking, that means a person who has completed the path of seeing. If you can do it, then good!

The second is middling but is the best for the ordinary practitioner. It means to do a dedication by following and hence training in the way that has been shown by the realized beings, the buddhas and bodhisatvas. You visualize the buddhas and bodhisatvas before you and think like this, "All of the buddhas and bodhisatvas do dedications and prayers of aspiration for the sake of all sentient beings. I also will do as they do. I put all of the virtue, all of the merit, that I have accumulated (by whatever virtuous deed you have just done, whether meditation on shamatha, vipashyana, whether doing circumambulation, charity, etcetera) together with the virtue accumulated by all the buddhas and all other sentient beings and then, just as all of you buddhas and bodhisatvas have dedicated it, so I too dedicate it for the sake of all sentient beings. May all sentient beings obtain this virtue. Now every sentient being has gained the causes of obtaining the rank of a buddha." Once you have made that conventional dedication, train yourself further by rousing whatever understanding you have attained so far that the dedicator, yourself, is empty and the object of the dedication, sentient beings, equally are empty, and that the act of dedication also is totally empty, and rest your mind on that.

The third was named in various ways by the Buddha in the *Prajnaparamita Sutra*. One way was "dedication mixed with poison". The name refers to dedication done in general with a mind that is not directly realizing the emptiness of the sphere of the three, a mind which is not directly perceiving its own essence, but which dedicates whatever virtue has been accumulated thinking, "I dedicate this to sentient beings; may they have it; may they receive it". It is just that much and no more. Do not think, because of the name, that this kind of dedication has no value. To the contrary, it is a very valuable thing to do, it is just that it cannot bring the immeasurable, limitless benefit of the first kind of dedication which is done with the direct perception of emptiness.

What is the point of doing a dedication? The main point is that it prevents the merit you have created from going to waste. What does it mean that merit could go to waste? There are four causes that exhaust merit:

1. Arising of anger
2. Lack of humility
3. Regret
4. Ripening

The Buddha explained that a moment of anger destroys aeons of merit. However, if the merit has been dedicated, the anger cannot touch it. If you are very proud and overbearing, constantly belittling others and saying you are better than they, then this also destroys merit. Again, if the merit has been dedicated, this negativity cannot touch it. If you regret something virtuous done, this tends to damage the virtue connected with it; it makes it diminish to a greater or lesser degree. However, if the virtuous action is followed by dedication before the regret sets in, then, no matter how much regret you have later, the merit will not be affected. Finally, merit does come to fruition sooner or later. If you do not dedicate the merit properly, it will bring its result at some point in the future and then will be finished. The good karma ripens into its result and then is finished with. However, if the merit is dedicated properly, it brings results but is never exhausted. Not only that but, if dedicated properly, it doesn't merely stay the same but steadily increases over time, just like money put in an account in a good bank pays interest and steadily increases in value as time passes.

Dedication is, all in all, a seal that is put on virtuous activity. By putting that seal there, the merit cannot be damaged or destroyed and in fact, if the dedication is done properly, as described above, creates a merit account that steadily increases in value.

GLOSSARY

Actuality, Tib. gnas lugs: A key term in both sūtra and tantra and one of a pair of terms, the other being "apparent reality" (Tib. snang lugs). The two terms are used when determining the reality of a situation. The actuality of any given situation is how (lugs) the situation actuality sits or is present (gnas); the apparent reality is how (lugs) any given situation appears (snang) to an observer. Something could appear in many different ways, depending on the circumstances at the time and on the being perceiving it but, regardless of those circumstances, it will always have its own actuality of how it really is. This term is frequently used in Mahāmudrā and Great Completion teachings to mean the fundamental reality of any given phenomenon or situation before any deluded mind alters it and makes it appear differently.

Adventitious, Tib. glo bur: This term has the connotations of popping up on the surface of something and of not being part of that thing. Therefore, even though it is often translated as "sudden", that only conveys half of the meaning. In Buddhist literature, something adventitious comes up as a surface event and disappears again precisely because it is not actually part of the thing on whose surface it appeared. It is frequently used in relation to the afflictions because they pop up on the surface of the mind of buddha-nature but are not part of the buddha-nature itself.

Affliction, Skt. kleśha, Tib. nyon mongs: This term is usually translated as emotion or disturbing emotion, etcetera, but the Buddha was very specific about the meaning of this word. When the Buddha referred to the emotions, meaning a movement of mind, he did not refer to them as such but called them "kleśha" in Sanskrit, meaning exactly "affliction". It is a basic part of the Buddhist teaching that emotions afflict beings, giving them problems at the time and causing more problems in the future.

Alertness, Tib. shes bzhin: Alertness is a specific mental event that occurs in dualistic mind. It and another mental event, mindfulness, are the two functions of mind that must be developed in order to develop shamatha or one-pointedness of mind. In that context, mindfulness is what remembers the object of the concentration and holds the mind to it while alertness is the mind watching the situation to ensure that the mindfulness is not lost. If distraction does occur, alertness will know it and will inform the mind to re-establish mindfulness again.

Arousing the mind, Tib. sems bskyed: This is a technical term nearly always used to mean "arousing the enlightenment mind", though it is occasionally used to refer to the deliberate production of other types of mind, for example renunciation. There are two types of arousing the mind—fictional and superfactual; see under fictional enlightenment mind and superfactual enlightenment mind.

Awareness, Skt. jñā, Tib. shes pa: "Awareness" is always used in our translations to mean the basic knower of mind or, as Buddhist teaching itself defines it, "a general term for any registering mind", whether dualistic or non-dualistic. Hence, it is used for both samsaric and nirvanic situations; for example, consciousness (Tib. rnam par shes pa) is a dualistic form of awareness, whereas rigpa, wisdom (Tib. ye shes), and so on are non-dualistic forms of awareness.

Bliss, luminosity, and no-thought, Tib. bde gsal mi rtog pa: A person who actually practises meditation will have signs of that practice appear as various types of temporary experience. Most commonly, three types of experience are met with: bliss, luminosity, and no-thought. Bliss is an ease of body or mind or both, luminosity is the knowing factor of mind, and no-thought is an absence of thought that happens in the mind. The three are usually mentioned when discussing the passing experiences that arise because of practising meditation but there is also a way of describing them as final experiences of realization.

Note that this has often been called "bliss, clarity, and no-thought" but that makes the mistake that the word for luminosity has been abbreviated in this phrase and mistaken by translators to mean something else.

Bodhicitta, Tib. byang chub sems: See under enlightenment mind.

Bodhisatva, Tib. byang chub sems dpa': A bodhisatva is a person who has engendered the bodhichitta, enlightenment mind, and, with that as a basis, has undertaken the path to the enlightenment of a truly complete buddha specifically for the welfare of other beings. Note that, despite the common appearance of "bodhisattva" in Western books on Buddhism, the Tibetan tradition has steadfastly maintained since the time of the earliest translations that the correct spelling is bodhisatva; see under satva and sattva.

Bodhisatva mahasattva, Skt. bodhisatva mahāsattva, Tib. byang chub sems dpa' sems dpa' chen po: In general, "bodhisatva" refers to *satva*, a being, who is on the path to *bodhi*, truly complete enlightenment, and "mahāsattva" refers to a person who is *mahā* at a greater level of *sattva* being, a higher kind of person. Thus, the usual explanation of *bodhisatva mahāsattva* is that it means "a being on the path to truly complete enlightenment, one who is a great type of being because of his intention to reach truly complete enlightenment for the sake of all sentient beings.

However, there is also a second, less common explanation, in which "mahāsattva" does not mean a great being in general but has the specific meaning of those bodhisatvas who, amongst all bodhisatvas, have attained a very great level of being. In this case, it particularly refers to bodhisatvas who have achieved and are dwelling on the highest bodhisatva levels, the eighth to tenth bodhisatva levels. Unlike bodhisatvas at all levels below that, these bodhisatvas have attained such a high level of purity that they cannot regress to a lower level. Their level of attainment is enormous and with it, they have many qualities which are very similar to those of a buddha. It is important to know of this second understanding of "bodhisatva mahāsattva", because when it is used with that meaning, it says something about the bodhisatvas being mentioned. For example, when any of the eight heart-sons of the Buddha are mentioned, they are often referred to as bodhisatva mahāsattvas to indicate their extreme level of attainment. In that case, they specifically are the bodhisatvas above all other bodhisatvas, ones who are close to truly complete enlightenment.

Clinging, Tib. zhen pa: In Buddhism, this term refers specifically to the twofold process of dualistic mind mis-taking things that are not true, not pure, as true, pure, etcetera and then, because of seeing them as highly desirable even though they are not, attaching itself to or clinging to those things. This type of clinging acts as a kind of glue that keeps a person joined to the unsatisfactory things of cyclic existence because of mistakenly seeing them as desirable.

Complete purity, rnam dag: This term refers to the quality of a buddha's mind, which is completely pure compared to a sentient being's mind. The mind of a being in saṃsāra has its primordially pure nature covered over by the muck of dualistic mind. If the being practises correctly, the impurity can be removed and mind can be returned to its original state of complete purity.

Confusion, Tib. 'khrul pa: In Buddhism, this term mostly refers to the fundamental confusion of taking things the wrong way that happens because of fundamental ignorance, although it can also have the more general meaning of having lots of thoughts and being confused about it. In the first case, it is defined like this "Confusion is the appearance to rational mind of something being present when it is not" and refers, for example, to seeing an object, such as a table, as being truly present, when in fact it is present only as mere, interdependent appearance.

Consciousness, Skt. vijñāna, Tib. rnam shes: The term means "awareness of superficies". A consciousness is a dualistic (jñā) awareness which simply registers a certain type of (vi) superfice, for example, an eye consciousness by definition registers only the superficies of visual form. A very important point is that the addition of the "vi" to the basic term (jñā) for awareness conveys the sense of a less than perfect way of being aware. This is not a wisdom awareness which knows every superfice in an utterly uncomplicated way but a limited type of awareness which is restricted to knowing one kind of superfice or another and which is part of the complicated—and highly unsatisfactory process—called (dualistic) mind. Note that this definition, which is a crucial part of understanding the role of consciousness in samsaric being, is fully conveyed by the Sanskrit and Tibetan terms but not at all by the English term.

Cyclic existence: See under saṃsāra.

Dharmakaya, Skt. dharmakāya, Tib. chos sku: In the general teachings of Buddhism, this refers to the mind of a buddha, with "dharma" meaning reality and "kāya" meaning body. In the Thorough Cut practice of Great Completion it additionally has the special meaning of being the means by which one rapidly imposes liberation on oneself.

Dharmata, Skt. dharmatā, Tib. chos nyid: This is a general term meaning the way that something is, and can be applied to anything at all; it is similar in meaning to "actuality" *q.v.* For example, the dharmatā of water is wetness and the dharmatā of the becoming bardo is a place where beings are in a samsaric, or becoming mode, prior to entering a nature bardo. It is used frequently in Tibetan Buddhism to mean "the dharmatā of reality" but that is a specific case of the much larger meaning of the term. To read texts which use this term successfully, one has to understand that the term has a general meaning and then see how that applies in context.

Discursive thought, Skt. vikalpa, Tib. rnam rtog: This means more than just the superficial thought that is heard as a voice in the head. It includes the entirety of conceptual process that arises due to mind contacting any object of any of the senses. The Sanskrit and Tibetan literally mean "(dualistic) thought (that arises from the mind wandering among the) various (superficies *q.v.* perceived in the doors of the senses)".

Enlightenment mind, Skt. bodhicitta, Tib. byang chub sems: This is a key term of the Great Vehicle. It is the type of mind that is connected not with the lesser enlightenment of an arhat but the enlightenment of a truly complete buddha. As such, it is a mind which is connected with the aim of bringing all sentient beings to that same level of buddhahood. A person who has this mind has entered the Great Vehicle and is either a bodhisatva or a buddha.

It is important to understand that "enlightenment mind" is used to refer equally to the minds of all levels of bodhisatva on the path to buddhahood and to the mind of a buddha who has completed the path. Therefore, it is not "mind striving for enlightenment" as is so often translated, but "enlightenment mind", meaning that kind of mind which is connected with the full enlightenment of a truly complete buddha and which is present in all those who belong to the Great Vehicle. The term is used in the conventional Great Vehicle and also in the Vajra Vehicle. In the Vajra Vehicle, there are some special uses of the term where substances of the pure aspect of the subtle physical body are understood to be manifestations of enlightenment mind.

Entity, Tib. ngo bo: The entity of something is just exactly what that thing is. In English we would often simply say "thing" rather than entity. However, in Buddhism, "thing" has a very specific meaning rather than the general meaning that it has in English. It has become common to translate this term as "essence" *q.v.* However, in most cases "entity", meaning what a thing is rather than an essence of that thing, is the correct translation for this term.

Exaggeration, Tib. skur 'debs pa: In Buddhism, this term is used in two ways. Firstly, it is used in general to mean misunderstanding from the perspective that one has added more to one's understanding of something than needs to be there. Secondly, it is used specifically to indicate that dualistic mind always overstates or exaggerates whatever object it is examining. Dualistic mind always adds the ideas of solidity, permanence, singularity, and so on to everything it references via the concepts that it uses. Severing of exaggeration either means removal of these un-necessary understandings when trying to properly comprehend something or removal of the dualistic process altogether when trying to get to the non-dualistic reality of a phenomenon.

Fact, Skt. artha, Tib. don: "Fact" is that knowledge of an object that occurs to the surface of mind or wisdom. It is not the object but what the mind or wisdom understands as the object. Thus there are two usages of "fact": fact known to dualistic and non-dualistic minds. The higher tantras especially use "fact" to refer to the actual fact known in direct perception of actuality. Thus, there are phrases such as "in fact" which do not mean that the author is speaking truly about something but that whatever is about to be said is referring to actual fact as known to wisdom. A further complexity is that phrases such as "in fact" in those contexts are often abbreviations of "in superfact" *q.v.* This brings a further difficulty for the reader because "superfact" can be used in a general way to indicate directly perceived non-samsaric fact or can be used according to its specific definition (for which see superfact). In Buddhist tradition, problems like this are solved by having the text explained by one's teacher. That might not be possible for some readers, so uses of the word "fact" should be looked at carefully to see whether they are indicating fact in general or the factual situation of knowing reality in direct perception.

Fictional, Skt. saṃvṛtti, Tib. kun rdzob: This term is paired with the term "superfactual" *q.v.* In the past, these terms have been translated as "relative" and "absolute" respectively, but those translations are nothing like the original terms. These terms are extremely important in the Buddhist teaching so it is very important that they be corrected, but more than that, if the actual meaning of these terms is not presented, then the teaching connected with them cannot be understood.

The Sanskrit term saṃvṛtti means a deliberate invention, a fiction, a hoax. It refers to the mind of ignorance which, because of being obscured and so not seeing suchness, is not true but a fiction. The things that appear to that ignorance are therefore fictional. Nonetheless, the beings who live in this ignorance believe that the things that appear to them through the filter of ignorance are true, are real. Therefore, these beings live in fictional truth.

Fictional and superfactual saṃvṛiti, paramārtha: Fictional and superfactual are our greatly improved translations for "relative" and "absolute" respectively. Briefly, the original Sanskrit word for fiction means a deliberately produced *fiction* and refers to the world projected by a mind controlled by ignorance. The original word for superfact means "that *super*ior *fact* that appears on the surface of the mind of a noble one who has transcended saṃsāra" and refers to reality seen as it actually is. Relative and absolute do not convey this meaning at all and, when they are used, the meaning being presented is simply lost.

Fictional truth, Skt. saṃvṛtisatya, Tib. kun rdzob bden pa: See under fictional.

Fictional truth enlightenment mind, Tib. kun rdzob bden pa'i byang chub sems: One of a pair of terms explained in the Great Vehicle; the other is Superfactual Truth Enlightenment Mind. See under fictional truth and superfactual truth for information about those terms. Enlightenment mind is defined as two types. The fictional type is the conventional type: it is explained as consisting of love and great compassion within the framework of an intention to obtain truly complete enlightenment for the sake of all sentient beings. The superfactual truth type is the ultimate type: it is explained as the enlightenment mind that is directly perceiving emptiness.

Formative, Skt. saṃskāra, Tib. 'du byed. This term is usually translated as "formations", but a formation is the product of that which caused its formation, whereas this term refers to the agent which will cause a formation. The formatives, which are the contents of the fourth of the five aggregates, cause the production of a future set of aggregates for the mindstream involved. There are two types of formatives, ones which are a type of mind and ones which are not. The former includes all of the afflictions.

Great Completion, Tib. rdzogs pa chen po: Two main practices of reality developed in the Buddhist traditions of ancient India and then came to Tibet: Great Completion (Mahāsandhi) and Great Seal (Mahāmudrā). Great Completion and Great Seal are names for reality and names for a practice that directly leads to that reality. Their ways of describing reality and their practices are very similar. The Great Completion teachings are the pinnacle teachings of the tantric teachings of Buddhism that first came into Tibet with Padmasambhava and his peers and were later kept alive in the Nyingma (Earlier Ones) tradition. The Great Seal practice came into Tibet later and was held in the Sakya and Kagyu lineages. Later again, the Great Seal was held by the Gelugpa lineage, which obtained its transmissions of the instructions from the Sakya and Kagyu lineages.

It is popular nowadays to call Great Completion by the name Great Perfection, though that is a mistake. The original name Mahāsandhi refers to that one space of reality in which all things come together. Thus it means "completeness" or "completion" as the Tibetans chose to translate it and does not imply or contain the sense of "perfection".

Great Vehicle, Skt. mahāyāna, Tib. theg pa chen po: The Buddha's teachings as a whole can be summed up into three vehicles where a vehicle is defined as that which can carry a person to a certain destination. The first vehicle, called the Lesser Vehicle, contains the teachings designed to get an individual moving on the spiritual path through showing the unsatisfactory state of cyclic existence and an emancipation from that. However, that path is only concerned with personal emancipation and fails to take account of all of the beings that there are in existence. There used to be eighteen schools of Lesser Vehicle in India but the only one surviving nowadays is the Theravāda of south-east Asia. The Greater Vehicle is a step up from that. The Buddha explained that it was great in comparison to the Lesser Vehicle for seven reasons. The first of those is that it is concerned with attaining the truly complete enlightenment of a truly complete buddha for the sake of every sentient being where the Lesser Vehicle is concerned only with a personal liberation that is not truly complete enlightenment and which is achieved only for the sake of that practitioner. The Great Vehicle has two divisions: a conventional form in which the path is taught in a logical, conventional way, and an unconventional form in which the path is taught in a very direct way. This latter vehicle is called the Vajra Vehicle because it takes the innermost, indestructible (vajra) fact of reality of one's own mind as the vehicle to enlightenment.

Kagyu, Tib. bka' brgyud: There are four main schools of Buddhism in Tibet—Nyingma, Kagyu, Sakya, and Gelug. Nyingma is the oldest school dating from about 800 C.E. Kagyu and Sakya both appeared in the 12th century C.E. Each of these three schools came directly from India. The Gelug school came later and did not come directly from India but came from the other three. The Nyingma school holds the tantric teachings called Great Completion (Dzogchen); the other three schools hold the tantric teachings called Mahāmudrā. Kagyu practitioners often join Nyingma practice with their Kagyu practice and Kagyu teachers often teach both, so it is common to hear about Kagyu and Nyingma together.

Kaya, Skt. kāya, Tib. sku: The Sanskrit term means a functional or coherent collection of parts, similar to the French "corps", and hence also comes to mean "a body". It is used in Tibetan Buddhist texts specifically to distinguish bodies belonging to the enlightened side from ones belonging to the samsaric side.

Enlightened being in Buddhism is said to be comprised of one or more kayas. It is most commonly explained to consist of one, two, three, four, or five kāyas, though it is pointed out that there are infinite aspects to enlightened being and therefore it can also be said to consist of an infinite number of kāyas. In fact, these descriptions of enlightened being consisting of one or more kāyas are given for the sake of understanding what is beyond conceptual understanding so should not be taken as absolute statements.

The most common description of enlightened being is that it is comprised of three kāyas: dharma, saṃbhoga, and nirmāṇakāyas. Briefly stated, the dharmakāya is the body of truth, the saṃbhogakāya is the body replete with the good qualities of enlightenment, and the nirmāṇakāya is the body manifested into the worlds of saṃsāra and nirvāṇa to benefit beings.

Dharmakāya refers to that aspect of enlightened being in which the being sees the truth for himself and, in doing so, fulfils his own needs for enlightenment. The dharmakāya is purely mind, without form. The remaining two bodies are summed up under the heading of rūpakāyas or form bodies manifested specifically to fulfil the needs of all un-enlightened beings. "Saṃbhogakāya" has been mostly translated as "body of enjoyment" or "body of rapture" but it is clearly stated in Buddhist texts on the subject that the name refers to a situation replete with what is useful, that is, to the fact that the saṃbhogakāya contains all of the good qualities of enlightenment as needed to benefit sentient beings. The saṃbhogakāya is extremely subtle and not accessible by most sentient beings; the nirmāṇakāya is a coarser manifestation which can reach sentient beings in many ways. Nirmāṇakāya should not be thought of as a physical body but as the capability to express enlightened being in whatever way is needed throughout all the different worlds of sentient beings. Thus, as much as it appears as a supreme buddha who shows the dharma to beings, it also appears as anything needed within sentient beings' worlds to give them assistance.

The three kāyas of enlightened being is taught in all levels of Buddhist teaching. It is especially important in Mahāmudrā and Great Completion and is taught there in a unique and very profound way.

The four kāyas usually refers to the three kāyas defined above with the addition of the svabhāvikakāya, the most essential body. This kāya is defined as the common emptiness of all three kāyas, that is, the fact that the three kāyas collectively are empty. The four kāyas occasionally refers to the three kāyas defined above with the addition of the mahāsukhakāya, the body of great bliss; the three kāyas collectively are enlightened being and therefore collectively are a body of the great bliss of enlightenment.

The five kāyas usually refers to the three kāyas plus the svabhāvikakāya to make four as defined above and then those four collectively are the mahāsukhakāya of great bliss.

Lesser Vehicle, Skt. hīnayāna, Tib. theg pa dman pa: See under Great Vehicle.

Luminosity or illumination, Skt. prabhāsvara, Tib. 'od gsal ba: The core of mind has two aspects: an emptiness factor and a knowing factor. The Buddha and many Indian religious teachers used "luminosity" as a metaphor for the knowing quality of the core of mind. If in English we would say "Mind has a knowing quality", the teachers of ancient India would say, "Mind has an illuminative quality; it is like a source of light which illuminates what it knows".

This term been translated as "clear light" but that is a mistake that comes from not understanding the etymology of the word. It does not refer to a light that has the quality of clearness (something that makes no sense, actually!) but to the illuminative property which is the nature of the empty mind.

Note also that in both Sanskrit and Tibetan Buddhist literature, this term is frequently abbreviated just to Skt. "vara" and Tib. "gsal ba" with no change of meaning. Unfortunately, this has been thought to be another word and it has then been translated with "clarity", when in fact it is just this term in abbreviation.

Mahamudra, Skt. mahāmudrā, Tib. phyag rgya chen po: Mahāmudrā is the name of a set of ultimate teachings on reality and also of the reality itself. This is explained at length in the book *Gampopa's Mahamudra: The Five-Part Mahamudra of the Kagyus* by Tony Duff, published by Padma Karpo Translation Committee, 2008, ISBN 978-9937-2-0607-5.

Mind, Skt. chitta, Tib. sems: There are several terms for mind in the Buddhist tradition, each with its own, specific meaning. This term is the most general term for the samsaric type of mind. It refers to the type of mind that is produced because of fundamental ignorance of enlightened mind. Whereas the wisdom of enlightened mind lacks all complexity and knows in a non-dualistic way, this mind of un-enlightenment is a very complicated apparatus that only ever knows in a dualistic way.

The Mahāmudrā and Great Completion teachings use the terms "entity of mind" and "mind's entity" to refer to what this complicated, samsaric mind is at core—the enlightened form of mind.

Mindfulness, Skt. smṛiti, Tib. dran pa: A particular mental event, one that has the ability to keep mind on its object. Together with alertness, it is one of the two causes of developing śhamatha. See under alertness for an explanation.

Nature Great Completion, Tib. rang bzhin rdzogs pa chen po: This is one of several names for Great Completion that emphasizes the path aspect of Great Completion. It is not "natural great completion" nor is it "the true nature Great Completion" as commonly seen. In terms of grammar, the first term is the noun "nature" not the adjective "natural". In terms of meaning, the noun nature is used because it refers to the nature aspect in particular of the three characteristics of the essence of mind—entity, nature, and un-stopped compassionate activity—used to describe Great Completion as experienced by the practitioner. Thus, this name refers to the approach taken by Great Completion and does not refer at all to Great Completion being a "natural" practice or its being connected with a "natural reality" or any of the many other, incorrect meanings that arise from the mistaken translation "natural Great Completion".

Noble one, Skt. ārya, Tib. 'phags pa: In Buddhism, a noble one is a being who has become spiritually advanced to the point that he has passed beyond cyclic existence. According to the Buddha, the beings in cyclic existence were ordinary beings, spiritual commoners, and the beings who had passed beyond it were special, the nobility.

Outflow, Skt. āsrāva, Tib. zag pa: The Sanskrit term means a bad discharge, like pus coming out of a wound. Outflows occur when wisdom loses its footing and falls into the elaborations of dualistic mind. Therefore, anything with duality also has outflows. This is sometimes translated as "defiled" or "conditioned" but these fail to capture the meaning. The idea is that wisdom can remain self-contained in its own unique sphere but, when it loses its ability to stay within itself, it starts to have leakages into dualism that are defilements on the wisdom. See also under un-outflowed.

Prajna, Skt. prajñā, Tib. shes rab: The Sanskrit term, literally meaning "best type of mind" is defined as that which makes correct distinctions between this and that and hence which arrives at correct understanding. It has been translated as "wisdom" but that is not correct because it is, generally speaking, a mental event belonging to dualistic mind where "wisdom" is used to refer to the non-dualistic knower of a buddha. Moreover, the main feature of prajñā is its ability to distinguish correctly between one thing and another and hence to arrive at a correct understanding.

Rational mind, Tib. blo: Rational mind is one of several terms for mind in Buddhist terminology. It specifically refers to a mind that judges this against that. With rare exception it is used to refer to samsaric mind, given that samsaric mind only works in the dualistic mode of comparing this versus that. Because of this, the term is mostly used in a pejorative sense to point out samsaric mind as opposed to an enlightened type of mind.

The Gelugpa tradition does have a positive meaning for this term and their documents will sometimes use it in that way; they make the claim that a buddha has an enlightened type of this mind. That is not wrong; one could refer to the ability of a buddha's wisdom to make a distinction between this and that with the term "rational mind". However, the Kagyu and Nyingma traditions in their Mahāmudrā and Great Completion teachings, reserve this term for the dualistic mind. In their teachings, it is the villain, so to speak, which needs to be removed from the practitioner's being in order to obtain enlightenment.

This term has been commonly translated simply as "mind" but that fails to identify this term properly and leaves it confused with the many other words that are also translated simply as "mind". It is not just another mind but is specifically the sort of mind that creates the situation of this and that (*ratio* in Latin) and hence, at least in the teachings of Kagyu and Nyingma, upholds the duality of saṃsāra. In that case, it is the very opposite of the essence of mind. Thus, this is a key term which should be noted and not just glossed over as "mind".

Realization, Tib. rtogs pa: Realization has a very specific meaning: it refers to correct knowledge that has been gained in such a way that the knowledge does not abate. There are two important points here. Firstly, realization is not absolute. It refers to the removal of obscurations, one at a time. Each time that a practitioner removes an obscuration, he gains a realization because of it. Therefore, there are as many levels of realization as there are obscurations. Maitreya, in the *Ornament of Manifest Realizations*, shows how the removal of the various obscurations that go with each of the three realms of samsaric existence produces realization.

Secondly, realization is stable or, as the Tibetan wording says, "unchanging". As Guru Rinpoche pointed out, "Intellectual knowledge is like a patch, it drops away; experiences on the path are temporary, they evaporate like mist; realization is unchanging".

A special usage of "realization" is found in the Essence Mahāmudrā and Great Completion teachings. There, realization is the term used to describe what happens at the moment when mindness is actually met during either introduction to or self-recognition of mindness. It is called realization because, in that glimpse, one actually directly sees the innate wisdom mind. The realization has not been stabilized but it is realization.

Refuge, Skt. śharaṇaṃ, Tib. bskyab pa: The Sanskrit term means "shelter", "protection from harm". Everyone seeks a refuge from the unsatisfactoriness of life, even if it is a simple act like brushing the teeth to prevent the body from decaying un-necessarily. Buddhists, after having thought carefully about their situation and who could provide a refuge from it which would be thoroughly reliable, find that three things— buddha, dharma, and saṅgha—are the only things that could provide that kind of refuge. Therefore, Buddhists take refuge in those Three Jewels of Refuge as they are called. Taking refuge in the Three Jewels is clearly laid out as the one doorway to all Buddhist practice and realization.

Rishi, Skt. ṛiṣhi, Tib. drang srong: A rishi is a holy man. The Sanskrit itself means one who has a sufficient level of spiritual accomplishment and knowledge to bring others along the path of spirituality properly. It was a common appellation in ancient India where there were many rishis. The Buddha was often referred to as "the rishi" meaning the rishi of all rishis or as the "great ṛiṣhi" meaning the greatest of all rishis.

Samsara, Skt. saṃsāra, Tib. 'khor ba: This is the most general name for the type of existence in which sentient beings live. It refers to the fact that they continue on from one existence to another, always within the enclosure of births that are produced by ignorance and experienced as unsatisfactory. The original Sanskrit means to be constantly going about, here and there. The Tibetan term literally means "cycling", because of which it is frequently translated into English with "cyclic existence" though that is not quite the meaning of the term.

Satva and sattva: According to the Tibetan tradition established at the time of the great translation work done at Samye under the watch of Padmasambhava not to mention one hundred and sixty-three of the greatest Buddhist scholars of Sanskrit-speaking India, there is a difference of meaning between the Sanskrit terms "satva" and "sattva", with satva meaning "an heroic kind of being" and "sattva" meaning simply "a being". According to the Tibetan tradition established under the advice of the Indian scholars mentioned above, satva is correct for the words Vajrasatva and bodhisatva, whereas sattva is correct for the words samayasattva, samādhisattva, and jñānasattva, and is also used alone to refer to any or all of these three satvas.

All Tibetan texts produced since the time of the great translations conform to this system and all Tibetan experts agree that this is correct, but Western translators of Tibetan texts have for the last few hundreds of years claimed that they know better and have "satva" to "sattva" in every case, causing confusion amongst Westerners confronted by the correct spellings. Recently, publications by Western Sanskrit scholars have been appearing in which these great experts finally admit that they were wrong and that the Tibetan system is and always has been correct!

Shamatha, Skt. śhamatha, Tib. gzhi gnas: This is the name of one of the two main practices of meditation used in the Buddhist system to gain insight into reality. This practice creates a one-pointedness of mind which can then be used as a foundation for development of the insight of the other practice, vipaśhyanā. If the development of śhamatha is taken through to completion, the result is a mind that sits stably on its object without any effort and a body which is filled with ease. Altogether, this result of the practice is called "the creation of workability of body and mind".

Sugata, Tib. bde bar gshegs pa: This term is one of many names for a buddha. It has the twofold meaning of someone who has gone on a good, pleasant, easy journey and who has arrived at a place which is good, pleasant, and full of ease. The meaning in relation to buddhahood is explained at length in *Unending Auspiciousness, the Sutra of the Recollection of the Noble Three Jewels* by Tony Duff, published by Padma Karpo Translation Committee, 2010, ISBN: 978-9937-8386-1-0.

Sugatagarbha, Tib. bde bar gshegs pa'i snying po: This one of a pair of terms for the potential existing in all sentient beings that makes the attainment of buddhahood possible, also called the buddha-nature. The other term is tathāgatagarbha. The sanskrit term "garbha" primarily means something which is potent but contained in an outer shell, like a seed, and is also used to mean a matrix or womb from which something can be produced. Both meanings are applicable.

Tibetans translated garbha with "snying po" which has many meanings but in this case means "an essence or core", which was their take on the meaning of buddha-nature. The meaning altogether is a seed contained within the obscurations of samsaric being, which makes it possible to become a sugata or tathāgatha, that is, a buddha.

Sugatagarbha has the same basic meaning as tathāgatagarbha but is a practical way of talking where tathagātagarbha is theoretical. Sugatagarbha is used when an author is talking about the practical realities of an essence that can be or is being developed into enlightened being. For example, in the sutras of the third turning of the wheel, the Buddha speaks of tathāgatagarbha when laying out the theory of buddha-nature but switches to sugatagarbha when speaking of wisdom as what is to be actually attained. Similarly, the tantras, which are mainly concerned with the practical attainment of wisdom mainly, use the term sugatagarbha and rarely use the term tathāgatagarbha. See also under sugata.

Superfactual, Skt. paramārtha, Tib. don dam: This term is paired with the term "fictional" *q.v.* In the past, the terms have been translated as "relative" and "absolute" respectively, but those translations are nothing like the original terms. These terms are extremely important in the Buddhist teaching so it is very important that their translations be corrected but, more than that, if the actual meaning of these terms is not presented, the teaching connected with them cannot be understood.

The Sanskrit term literally means "the fact for that which is above all others, special, superior" and refers to the wisdom mind possessed by those who have developed themselves spiritually to the point of having transcended saṃsāra. That wisdom is *superior* to an ordinary, un-developed person's consciousness and the *facts* that appear on its surface are superior compared to the facts that appear on the ordinary person's consciousness. Therefore, it is superfact or the holy fact, more literally. What this wisdom knows is true for the beings who have it, therefore what the wisdom sees is superfactual truth.

Superfactual truth, Skt. paramārthasatya, Tib. don dam bden pa: See under superfactual.

Superfactual truth enlightenment mind, Tib. don dam bden pa'i byang chub sems: This is one of a pair of terms; the other is Fictional Truth Enlightenment Mind *q.v.* for explanation.

Tathagatagarbha, Skt. tathāgatagarbha, Tib. de bzhin gshegs pa'i snying po: This means the garbha or seed of a tathāgata; see under sugatagarbha.

Temporary experience, Tib. nyams: The practice of meditation brings with it various experiences that happen simply because of doing meditation. These experiences are temporary experiences and not the final, unchanging experience, of realization.

The element, Skt. dhātu, Tib. khams. The Sanskrit term has many meanings; the meaning here is "a fundamental substance from which something else can be produced". When the Buddha explained the tathāgatagarbha or buddha nature in the third turning of the wheel, he used several names for it, each one showing a specific aspect of it. He called it the element with the meaning "that basis substance from which buddhahood can be produced". He called it "the type" meaning that it was the same sort of thing as buddhahood and therefore could lead to buddhahood; this term is also translated as "family" and "lineage". He also called it "the seed" meaning the seed of enlightenment. He also called it "the garbha"; see under sugatagarbha for the meaning.

Thorough Cut, Tib. khregs chod: One of the two practices of the innermost level of Great Completion practice. The other is

Direct Crossing. Thorough Cut is a practice in which the main point is to cut decisively through to Alpha Purity.

Three kayas: See under kaya.

Three Vehicles, theg pa gsum: The entire teachings of the Buddha can be summed up into three "vehicles". Each vehicle is a complete set of teachings that will take a person to a particular level of spiritual attainment. The first one, the Lesser Vehicle, is a set of teachings that will take a person out of cyclic existence but will not lead the person to full enlightenment. The second one, the Great Vehicle, is "great" relative to the Lesser Vehicle because it can lead a person to full enlightenment. The third vehicle, the Vajra Vehicle, also can lead a person to full enlightenment. The difference between the Great and Vajra Vehicles is that the first are exoteric teachings that are suitable for anyone whereas the second are esoteric teachings which are not. The Great Vehicle and the Vajra Vehicle both lead to the same attainment, but the first proceeds very gradually whereas the second is very fast. The Great Vehicle proceeds using the sūtra teachings of the Buddha whereas the Vajra Vehicle proceeds using the tantric teachings.

Unsatisfactoriness, Skt. duḥkha, Tib. sdug bngal: This term is usually translated into English with "suffering" but there are many problems with that. When the Buddha talked about the nature of samsaric existence, he said that it was unsatisfactory. He used the term "duḥkha", which includes actual suffering but means much more than that. Duḥkha is one of a pair of terms, the other being "sukha", which is usually translated as, but does not only mean, bliss. The real meaning of duḥkha is "everything on the side of bad"—not good, uncomfortable, unpleasant, not nice, and so on. Thus, it means "unsatisfactory in every possible way". The real meaning of its opposite, sukha, is "everything on the side of good"—not bad, comfortable, pleasant, nice, and so on.

Therefore, that he is completely liberated from the sufferings actually means that he has completely liberated himself from the unsatisfactoriness of samsara, which includes all types of suffering and happiness, too.

Vajra Vehicle, Skt. vajrayāna, Tib. rdo rje'i theg pa: See under Great Vehicle.

Vipashyana, Skt. vipaśhyanā, Tib. lhag mthong: This is the Sanskrit name for one of the two main practices of meditation needed in the Buddhist system for gaining insight into reality. The other one, śhamatha, keeps the mind focussed while this one looks piercingly into the nature of things.

Wisdom, Skt. jñāna, Tib. ye shes: This is a fruition term that refers to the kind of mind—the kind of knower—possessed by a buddha. Sentient beings do have this kind of knower but it is covered over by a very complex apparatus for knowing, that is, dualistic mind. If they practise the path to buddhahood, they will leave behind their obscuration and return to having this kind of knower.

The Sanskrit term has the sense of knowing in the most simple and immediate way. This sort of knowing is present at the core of every being's mind. Therefore, the Tibetans called it "the particular type of awareness which is there primordially". Because of the Tibetan wording it has often been called "primordial wisdom" in English translations, but that goes too far; it is just "wisdom" in the sense of the most fundamental knowing possible.

Wisdom does not operate in the same way as samsaric mind; it comes about in and of itself without depending on cause and effect. Therefore it is frequently referred to as "self-arising wisdom" *q.v.*

About the Author, Padma Karpo Translation Committee, and Their Supports for Study

I have been encouraged over the years by all of my teachers to pass on the knowledge I have accumulated in a lifetime dedicated to study and practice, primarily in the Tibetan tradition of Buddhism. On the one hand, they have encouraged me to teach. On the other, they are concerned that, while many general books on Buddhism have been and are being published, there are few books that present the actual texts of the tradition. Therefore they, together with a number of major figures in the Buddhist book publishing world, have also encouraged me to translate and publish high quality translations of individual texts of the tradition.

My teachers always remark with great appreciation on the extraordinary amount of teaching that I have heard in this life. It allows for highly informed, accurate translations of a sort not usually seen. Briefly, I spent the 1970's studying, practising, then teaching the Gelugpa system at Chenrezig Institute,

Australia, where I was a founding member and also the first Australian to be ordained as a monk in the Tibetan Buddhist tradition. In 1980, I moved to the United States to study at the feet of the Vidyadhara Chogyam Trungpa Rinpoche. I stayed in his Vajradhatu community, now called Shambhala, where I studied and practised all the Karma Kagyu, Nyingma, and Shambhala teachings being presented there and was a senior member of the Nalanda Translation Committee. After the vidyadhara's nirvana, I moved in 1992 to Nepal, where I have been continuously involved with the study, practise, translation, and teaching of the Kagyu system and especially of the Nyingma system of Great Completion. In recent years, I have spent extended times in Tibet with the greatest living Tibetan masters of Great Completion, receiving very pure transmissions of the ultimate levels of this teaching directly in Tibetan and practising them there in retreat. In that way, I have studied and practised extensively not in one Tibetan tradition as is usually done, but in three of the four Tibetan traditions—Gelug, Kagyu, and Nyingma—and also in the Theravada tradition, too.

With that as a basis, I have taken a comprehensive and long term approach to the work of translation. For any language, one first must have the lettering needed to write the language. Therefore, as a member of the Nalanda Translation Committee, I spent some years in the 1980's making Tibetan word-processing software and high-quality Tibetan fonts. After that, reliable lexical works are needed. Therefore, during the 1990's I spent some years writing the *Illuminator Tibetan-English Dictionary* and a set of treatises on Tibetan grammar, preparing a variety of key Tibetan reference works needed for the study and translation of Tibetan Buddhist texts, and giving our Tibetan software the tools needed to translate and research Tibetan texts. During this time, I also translated fulltime for various Tibetan gurus and ran the Drukpa Kagyu Heritage Project—at the time the largest project in Asia for the preservation of Tibetan Buddhist texts. With the dictionaries, grammar texts, and specialized software in place, and a wealth of knowledge, I turned my attention in the year 2000 to the translation and publication of important texts of Tibetan Buddhist literature.

Padma Karpo Translation Committee (PKTC) was set up to provide a home for the translation and publication work. The committee focusses on producing books containing the best of Tibetan literature, and, especially, books that meet the needs of practitioners. At the time of writing, PKTC has published a wide range of books that, collectively, make a complete program of study for those practising Tibetan Buddhism, and especially for those interested in the higher tantras. All in all, you will find many books both free and for sale on the PKTC web-site. Most are available both as paper editions and e-books.

It would take up too much space here to present an extensive guide to our books and how they can be used as the basis for a study program. However, a guide of that sort is available on the PKTC web-site, whose address is on the copyright page of this book and we recommend that you read it to see how this book fits into the overall scheme of PKTC publications. In short, given that this book is about the Kagyu approach to practice, including Mahāmudrā, other books of interest from PKTC would be:

- *Gampopa's Mahāmudrā, The Five-Part Mahāmudrā of the Kagyus*, a set of several texts showing the view of Mahāmudrā and how to practise it;
- *Drukchen Padma Karpo's Collected Works on Mahamudra*, the entire writings on Mahāmudrā of one of the most important Kagyu authors, with many details of the non-dual view;
- *The Bodyless Dakini Dharma: The Dakini Hearing Lineage of the Kagyus*, with several very early teachings on the view;
- *A Juggernaut of the Non-Dual View, Ultimate Teachings of the Second Drukchen Gyalwang Je*, a set of sixty-six teachings on the ultimate view by one of the early masters of the Drukpa Kagyu;
- *Maitrīpa's Writings on the View*, several teachings on the view from the "father of other emptiness";
- *Theory and Practice of Other Emptiness Taught Through Milarepa's Songs*, a complete explanation of the view of other emptiness given through two songs of Milarepa which are famous for their expositions of the non-dual view;
- *Dusum Khyenpa's Songs and Teachings*.

We make a point of including, where possible, the relevant Tibetan texts in Tibetan script in our books. We also make them available in electronic editions that can be downloaded free from our web-site, as discussed below. The Tibetan texts for this book have not been included because of size constraints.

Electronic Resources

PKTC has developed a complete range of electronic tools to facilitate the study and translation of Tibetan texts. For many years now, this software has been a prime resource for Tibetan Buddhist centres throughout the world, including in Tibet itself. It is available through the PKTC web-site.

The wordprocessor TibetDoc has the only complete set of tools for creating, correcting, and formatting Tibetan text according to the norms of the Tibetan language. It can also be used to make texts with mixed Tibetan and English or other languages. Extremely high quality Tibetan fonts, based on the forms of Tibetan calligraphy learned from old masters from pre-Communist Chinese Tibet, are also available. Because of their excellence, these typefaces have achieved a legendary status amongst Tibetans.

TibetDoc is used to prepare electronic editions of Tibetan texts in the PKTC text input office in Asia. After that, they are made available through the PKTC web-site. The electronic texts can be read, searched, and even made into an electronic library using either TibetDoc or our other software, TibetD Reader. Like TibetDoc, TibetD Reader is advanced software with many capabilities made specifically to meet the needs of reading and researching Tibetan texts. PKTC software is for purchase but we make a free version of TibetD Reader available for free download on the PKTC web-site.

A key feature of TibetDoc and Tibet Reader is that Tibetan terms in texts can be looked up on the spot using PKTC's electronic dictionaries. PKTC also has several electronic dictionaries—some Tibetan-Tibetan and some Tibetan-English—and a number of other reference works. The *Illuminator Tibetan-English Dictionary* is renowned for its completeness and accuracy.

This combination of software, texts, reference works, and dictionaries that work together seamlessly has become famous over the years. It has been the basis of many, large publishing projects within the Tibetan Buddhist community around the world for over thirty years and is popular amongst all those needing to work with Tibetan language or deepen their understanding of Buddhism through Tibetan texts.

Index

absence of deluded realities 59
absence of true existence .. xix,
    96, 99
actuality of emptiness ... 102
adventitious stains 10, 22
afflictions .. 13-15, 17, 48, 69,
    72, 125, 128, 143, 151
aggregates 115, 116, 151
agitation 83, 134, 135
alertness 67, 144, 156
all-knowing mind of a buddha
    6
analytical meditation 104, 105
appearance and emptiness
    .... 97, 112
appearances of confusion . 99
arousing bodhicitta xvi, 30, 35
arousing enlightenment mind
    .... iii, 35
assistant of shamatha 70
basic goodness 4
bodhicitta ... xvi, xvii, 30, 35,
    40, 44, 53, 54, 56, 145, 148
bodhisatvas . 11-13, 139, 140,
    146

bodily sensations 76
body and mind 65, 96
bottom-going-up approach xiii
buddha ... v, vi, x, xiii-xv, xviii,
    4-15, 17, 20-22, 27, 31, 35-40,
    45, 53, 55-57, 61, 65, 80, 85-
    89, 102-104, 109, 112, 113,
    122, 123, 139-141,
    144-149, 152, 154, 155,
    157-165, 180
buddha bodies 102
buddha wisdoms 102
buddhahood .. 4, 7, 8, 21, 31,
    55, 56, 88, 148, 161, 163, 165
cause of the distraction ... 69
Chogyam Trungpa Rinpoche
    .... vi, ix, 168, 180
coarse impermanence ... 109
common preliminaries ... 25
compassion ... 40, 41, 43-45,
    47-50, 52, 54, 56, 70, 151, 157
complete purity .. 4, 6, 45, 46,
    146, 147
complete session of meditation
    .... iii, xv-xvii, 22

complete session of practice
    .... xiii, xvi, xvii
completion stage .. 25, 27, 29
compounded things are impermanent 90, 109
confusion of rational mind   99
confusion of the path .. 27-29
consciousness 73, 97, 107,
    109, 111-114, 117-119, 144,
    147, 162, 163
conventional and unconventional xiii
conventional spirituality 21, 22
dedication .... iv, xvi, xvii, 30,
    139-141
development of spiritual qualities xii
development stage . 25, 27-30
dharmata 13, 18, 19, 148
direct sight of emptiness . 103
discursive thoughts ... 70, 72,
    81, 125, 126
distracted in meditation ... 69
distraction 60, 67, 69, 70,
    74, 75, 79, 81, 125-127, 135,
    144
Dolpopa Sherab Gyaltsen .. 9,
    10, 18, 21
dualistic kind of mind 86
dualistic mind .... x, xviii, 11,
    15, 50, 86, 88, 98, 122, 129,
    144, 146, 147, 149, 157,
    158, 165
dualistic process 73, 149
Dzogchen .... i, 153, 180
emptiness .. iv, xvii-xix, 17, 21,
    29, 36, 56, 59, 70, 87, 92, 97,
    99-105, 107, 112-116, 118,
    121-123, 125, 139, 140,
    151, 155, 170
emptiness of the phenomena
    99
enlightened core ... iii, xiv, 9,
    10, 18, 22, 62, 124
enlightenment ... iii, xiv, xvii,
    5, 7, 21, 27, 28, 35, 40, 44, 45,
    47, 53-57, 59, 71, 112, 144-
    146, 148, 149, 151-156, 158,
    163, 164
equipoise 65, 67, 122
essence of mind .. 5, 7, 11, 70,
    123, 124, 129, 139, 158
factual reality 53, 88
fictional enlightenment mind
    .... 55-57, 144
fictional level of reality ... 53,
    87, 109
fictional reality 37, 53, 87
fictional situation 86
fictional truth 87-89, 110-
    112, 117, 122, 123, 150, 151,
    163
first step of Buddhist practice 7
five aggregates . 115, 116, 151
five skandhas 115
Four Dharmas of Gampopa
    .... xv, 30
Four Immeasurables 49, 51, 52
four schools of Buddhist philosophy .... iv, 89
four sets of one hundred thousand 26
Four Truths of the Noble
    Ones 36, 38

INDEX

fundamental confusion ... 27, 99, 147
fundamental ignorance ... 85-89, 108, 147, 156
fundamental reality ... xi, xvii-19, 143
Gampopa ..... xv-xvii, 25-30, 156, 170
Gampopa's Mahamudra xvi, 156
Great Completion .... vi, xiv, 30, 59, 61, 62, 66-68, 123, 124, 130, 135, 136, 143, 148, 151-153, 155-159, 163, 168
Great Vehicle ... xvi, xvii, 19, 20, 30, 40, 49, 89, 112, 113, 115, 148, 149, 151-153, 155, 164, 165
ground of your being ... 7, 8
Hevajra Tantra 21
Highest Continuum Commentary 13
how to develop prajna 88
ignorance 19, 85-89, 96, 108, 147, 150, 151, 156, 160
illuminating quality ... 60, 61
impermanent ... xviii, xix, 87, 89-91, 93, 108-110, 112-114, 117
impure appearances ... 27-29, 102, 103
independence ... xix, 89, 111
independent entities xviii
insight .. iii, x-xii, xvii, xix, 54, 59, 61, 67, 85, 88, 107, 129, 161, 165
intellectual investigation v
interdependent arisings .. xviii, 120
interdependent reality 98
invention of rational mind xix
Kadampa lineage xvi
Kadampa teaching xvii
Kagyu-Nyingma .... i, vi
Lesser Vehicle ... xviii, 49, 89, 107, 112, 113, 152, 153, 155, 164
Longchen Rabjam 72
loving-kindness ... 40, 43-45, 47-50, 52, 54, 56, 70
loving-kindness and compassion ... 40, 43-45, 47-50, 52, 54, 56, 70
luminosity 10, 19, 22, 68, 132-134, 136, 137, 145, 155
luminosity nature of mind 134
luminosity-dharmakaya 10
Mahamudra ... xiv, xvi, 30, 59, 61, 62, 67, 68, 80, 123, 124, 130, 135-137, 156, 170
main practice of meditation 27
matter . 10, 43, 46, 74, 79, 93, 97, 98, 117, 126, 128, 133, 141
meditation on the essence of mind 123
meditative state of mind .. 67
Mind Only 113, 114, 118, 158
mindfulness .. 67, 70-79, 127, 144, 156
Mingyur Rinpoche ... vi-viii, 28
modern physics viii
moment of consciousness

.... 118, 119
moments of consciousness
  . 97, 107, 111-114, 117, 118
Mountain Dharma: An Ocean of Definitive Meaning 9
multiplicity .. xviii, 89, 95, 96, 110, 111
natural illuminating quality of the mind 61
non-distracted and non-meditation style 68
non-distraction .. 75, 81, 125, 127
non-dualistic way of knowing x
non-meditation 68, 130, 132-134, 137
object of the eye 71
object of the senses 69, 74, 133
obscurity of mind 7
ordinary people 5
Ornament of the Great Vehicle Sutras 20
outflows 11, 157
Padmasambhava . vii, 152, 160
Particularists 113, 118
partless atoms 114, 115
permanent entities xviii
permanent, singular, and independent 108, 112
personal self 112, 113, 115, 116
Phagmo Drupa xv
phenomena and beings ... 87
poor man's house 10, 11, 13, 14
prajna examines for superfactual truth 96
prajna examines the fictional truth 89

prajñā 157
present moment ... 91, 97, 98, 114, 118, 119, 121, 122, 132
pure essence 8
rational mind . ix-xi, xviii, xix, 25-27, 53, 86, 87, 89-91, 95, 96, 98, 99, 108, 147, 158
real peace 3
resting meditation .. 104, 105
rough experiences 83
saṅgha 159
Sautrantika 113
scientific theory ...... viii, ix
self-cherishing . 41, 43, 44, 55
self-grasping 40, 56, 57
Sending and Taking 54, 55, 57
sending-taking 54
sense objects 70-72, 74, 78, 125
seven key points of body .. 65
shamatha .... i, iii, vii, 27, 30, 54, 59-62, 67-71, 80, 81, 88, 104, 105, 123-130, 135-137, 140, 144, 161
shamatha and vipashyana unified together 68
shamatha with reference 68, 69
shamatha without reference 67, 68, 130
shamatha-vipashyana .. vii, 27, 30, 124, 128, 137
singularity .. xviii, xix, 89, 95, 149
sinking 83, 134, 135
sinking and agitation 135
six paramitas 40
smooth experiences ... 81-83
solidity of the external world x

space and time .... x-xii
spiritual development 5
spiritual path .. vi, xiv, 22, 152
spiritually advanced beings
.... 36, 87
stability of mind 88
steps in the development of
shamatha 80
subtle impermanence ... 109
sub-atomic particles 98
sugatagarbha . 6-8, 45, 46, 54,
161-163
superfactual enlightenment
mind 56, 144
superfactual truth . 87, 88, 96,
111, 117, 118, 122, 123, 151,
163
superior reality 87
taking refuge . iii, xvi, xvii, 30,
35, 39, 57, 159
tantras . x, 21, 22, 27, 28, 130,
149, 162, 169
tathagatagarbha ... 11, 12, 14,
15, 18, 20, 22, 163
Tathagatagarbha Sutra 11
temporary experiences 82, 163
the actual situation . xviii, 86-
88, 100
the benefits of meditating on
emptiness 103
the community 39, 180
the essence of mind 5, 7,
123, 124, 129, 139, 158
the four mind reversers ... 26
The Mahaparinirvana .. 14, 15
the nature of your own mind
.... 68, 124

the stock market 94, 95
the Three Jewels . xvii, 39, 159
the two truths and emptiness iv
Three Jewels .... xvii, 35, 39,
159, 161
three mistakes xviii
three mis-apprehensions .. 89,
108
Three Vehicle journey ... xiv
three wrong perceptions .. 89
Tibetan Buddhism . v, vi, xiii,
xiv, 22, 25, 148, 169, 180
Tibetan tradition ...... vi, 44,
145, 160, 167, 168
top-down approach xiii
Trilogy on Resting Up in Absorption 72
true existence . xix, 96, 97, 99
truly complete buddha ... 12,
17, 40, 53, 112, 145, 148, 149,
152
truly existent .. xix, 87, 97, 99-
101, 103, 108, 117
truth of cessation 36, 38
truth of source 36-38
truth of the path 38
truth of unsatisfactoriness
.... 36, 37
Tsoknyi Rinpoche . vii, 28, 180
two-fold emptiness 114
uncommon preliminaries . 25
unconventional spirituality
.... 21, 22
unsatisfactoriness .. 4, 13, 35-
38, 45, 88, 89, 159, 164, 165
unsatisfactory existence ... xix
Vajra Vehicle .. iv, xiv, xvi, 25,

28-30, 67, 112, 113, 123, 149, 153, 164, 165
Vajra Vehicle journey xvi
vajra vehicle meditations on reality iv
Vajrasatva 133, 160
vipaśhyanā 85, 161, 165
visual forms and colours .. 71
Western scientists 98
what is prajna 85
wild monkey 3
wisdom 11, 12, 19, 26, 27, 29, 55, 145, 147, 149, 150, 156-159, 162, 163, 165, 180
with reference and without reference 67
your basic nature 4

www.ingramcontent.com/pod-product-compliance
Lightning Source LLC
Chambersburg PA
CBHW022009160426
43197CB00007B/342